Princes and Ogres
Integration of Psyche and Soul

Millennial Mind Publishing
An imprint of American Book Publishing
5442 So. 900 East, #146
Salt Lake City, UT 84117-7204
www.american-book.com
Printed in the United States of America on acid-free paper.

Princes and Ogres: Integration of Psyche and Soul

Designed by Jana Rade, design@american-book.com

Library of Congress Cataloging-in-Publication Data

Mordasini, Don.
Princes and ogres : integration of psyche and soul / Don Mordasini.
p. cm.
ISBN-13: 978-1-58982-825-4 (acid-free paper)
ISBN-10: 1-58982-825-9 (acid-free paper)
1. Self-actualization (Psychology) 2. Awareness. 3. Wisdom. 4. Desire. 5. Self-realization. I. Title.
BF637.S4M637 2011
158--dc23
2011018461

Special Sales

These books are available at special discounts for bulk purchases. Special editions, including personalized covers, excerpts of existing books, and corporate imprints, can be created in large quantities for special needs. For more information e-mail info@american-book.com.

Princes and Ogres
Integration of Psyche and Soul

Don Mordasini

Introduction

The focus of this book is to help you, the reader, to realize your fullest potential. You contain within yourself the seeds of ultimate fulfillment. Peace, love, harmony, charity, personal fulfillment, and the flowering of the Shining Self are buried within you. Your life is a very precious and special experience. You have the potential to take yourself to the heights of human and even godly experience. However, no matter how sincere our desire or diligent our efforts, we must know the thoughts and emotions below our conscious awareness that prevent us from achieving our dreams. I call these thoughts and emotions the "ogre" because it guards entrance to the treasures within.

Long before the written word or its widespread dissemination, sages roamed the ancient world, imparting wisdom and knowledge through the art of storytelling, poetry, and song. Rather than teach lessons that might be forgotten, the sages created the time-honored device of wisdom stories, which were easily remembered and retold, such as the one below.

God had completed his creation including man and sat puzzled for a moment. He thought to himself, "Man is part of Me. How shall I lead man to this knowledge? If I withhold the joy of discovery, man may never plumb the depths of his being to know his complete nature. It would be better if I do not make his nature obvious, less he tastes a bit of divinity and stops short of exploring the infinite nature of himself. I think I will enter the body through the suture of the skull. I know that if tongue spoke, breath breathed, eyes saw, skin touched, mind thought, it would immediately know Me."

God then opened the suture of the skull, and entered through the gate, which is called the Gate of Joy. He found three places in the body where he could live, three conditions where He could move: waking, dreaming, and sleeping.

He entered the body, named its various parts, wondered if there could be anything there not Himself, and rejoiced there was nothing but Himself.

Two thousand years ago this story was told by wise men, or rishis, who had discovered God in the innermost depths of their being and taught from personal transcendent experience. Those who listened understood the message: you have a soul; you are a spark of the divine, wake up and discover this truth for yourself. This story, which is called *God Seeks a Home*, is woven into Chapter Three's subject of man discovering godhead, or soul.

Such stories reminded early man that his human being-ness contained a soul that was a microcosm of the Creator. Long after these itinerant sages moved on, the illiterate villagers remembered the lessons they were taught. They told their children these stories, and their children passed them on through countless generations until they found their way into written form a few thousand years ago. We remember stories, songs, and poems. The sages of old knew their lessons could best be learned when woven into the fabric of an interesting story or recited in a poem.

I came across this story recently in a set of scriptures known as the *Upanishads*, which comprise man's earliest written spiritual discourse. I was never exposed to this type of teaching until about fifteen years ago. After years of spiritual search, I met my guru, Shri Anandi Ma, and became her student. As I sat at her feet, she would discuss a topic and suddenly begin singing an ancient poem in Sanskrit. After she translated it she would tell us a story to underline the message being conveyed. I found this method of storytelling very effective in nurturing my spiritual life. As I studied the works of other spiritual teachers, East and West, I found they all used wisdom stories to teach their students.

As a psychotherapist I have found that many of these stories contain a universal wisdom that is as helpful today as it was six thousand years ago. I was astonished by the keen psychological insight of these ancient stories when I began to outline this present work using psychological themes to correlate them with wisdom stories. Of course in ancient times, there was no separation between spiritual wisdom and what we've come to call psychological understanding. Marie-Louise von Franz, the great Jungian commentator, revealed the psychological insight of many ancient fairy tales. And Robert Bly in his wonderful *Iron John* brought this approach to an even wider audience.

I have found that we can accelerate our personal growth by blending the best of modern psychology with ancient spiritual wisdom. Although the rishis' knowledge of human behavior was truly astounding, they didn't necessarily give us the tools needed to contend with today's wily characters, ego traps, and material lifestyles. We need to truly know ourselves and understand our ego's weaknesses and strengths to create what I like to call a "healthy ego." By working psychologically to understand our self and by following the wisdom of the ages, both disciplines harmonize and shorten the path to wholeness, simultaneously dealing with such thorny issues like phobias, obsessions, and compulsions.

The teachings guide us so we don't lose our way. In this book I use stories and poems from the Hindu, Buddhist, Christian, Judaic, American Indian, and Islamic traditions as well as the Desert Fathers to illustrate the psycho/spiritual understanding I try to convey.

Although the stories and poems contain universal wisdom, I found that they are best illustrated for a modern audience by using vignettes taken from people's lives in today's world struggling with similar universal issues. Many have applied the tools of modern psychology to curb ego excesses and create harmony in their lives, which is the way of the ancient Tao.

These stories, poems, and vignettes are interesting to read and hold our attention, but more importantly they increase our awareness and expand our consciousness. We need to face ourselves with absolute openness and honesty. When we don't recognize the wiles of our ego, which I allude to as our ogres, we tend to objectify it and project it onto other people demonizing or "ogreizing" them. The demons of the world become our focus. Chapter Four's *Sticky Hair* discusses the ogre within each of us and how we project our ogre onto others. The only battle we can fight is the battle within ourselves. This battle is our inner war. The holy war is the conflict between the needs of the ego and the emergence of the Self. The *jihad*, the *devil*, and the *axis of evil* are all inside of us. When we don't understand this dynamic, we impede our spiritual progress and create discrimination, hatred, intolerance, and division in the world. *Sticky Hair* becomes the radical Islam, the intolerant fundamentalist, and the nuclear axis of evil because we project the shadowy parts of our personality onto them.

The Bhagavad Gita, the Hindu Bible, stages its teaching on a battlefield as opposing armies that face off against each other, as a metaphor for the inner battle to claim the Shining Self in all its fullness and grandeur. The perennial literature is replete with epic stories such as the *Gita* that remind us over and over that change must come from within us. Mahatma Gandhi reminded us of this truth when he said, "You must be the change you wish to see in the world."

Today we need to blend such psychological insight with the spiritual wisdom handed down from the ancient sages. We need wholeness and transcendental wisdom to solve our problems and, mend our divisions, to help us and experience peace, quietude, respect, love, and charity for ourselves and others. Our thoughts and emotions are vibrations, nothing more. What resonates inside us resonates outside us. Our inside reality becomes our outside reality. We create our inner world, and we create our outer world. The perennial wisdom tells us to master ourselves, and as we do, our planet will benefit.

A Sufi teacher said, "Within you is that which completely transcends the entire universe."[1] The point is that the god within us cannot be confined or contained in the universe or a thousand universes that make up all of creation.

A thirteenth century Christian mystic said, "God gives

---

[1]   Sheik Muzaff

birth to the Son as you and me, as each one of us . . . I find in this divine birth that God and I are the same, in this birth I have become the motionless cause of all that moves." [2]

East or West, the perennial teaching is the same. Spiritual wisdom is contained in our soul (godhead) deep within our self. This book not only encourages you to plumb the depths of your human and spiritual nature but through story, poem, and vignettes show the way to the Shining Self.

Princes and Ogres begins with basic psychological and wisdom concepts that are important to grasp before we progress further. I suggest reading each chapter and fully understanding its content before moving on to the next stage. The first few chapters lay the framework for later chapters, which allow a natural expansion of the self, both human and divine.

---

[2] Meister Eckhart

Contents

Chapter One
Perception and Shaping Reality

Ahmad had acquired a beautiful parrot at the bazaar many years ago and proudly displayed it to his friends at every opportunity. He was about to travel from Baghdad to India on business, and although he had made this trip many times, he was now deeply saddened at the thought of leaving his parrot.

Finally, on the day of his departure, Ahmad reluctantly decided to ask the parrot if he had any messages to send to his kinsman in India. The parrot thought for a while and said, "Ahmad, if you would be so kind, please tell my cousins that I have been confined in a cage."

The merchant promised to deliver this message and set out on his trip. On arriving in India, he encountered a flock of parrots and duly told them the message from their cousin in Baghdad. On hearing it, one of them fell down dead. Ahmad was annoyed with his parrot for having sent such a fateful message, and upon his return home rebuked him. But as soon as the parrot heard the merchant's tale, he too fell down dead in his cage.

After lamenting his death, Ahmad took the parrot out of the cage and threw him on a trash heap; but to his surprise, the bird immediately recovered and flew away. In parting he told Ahmad that the Hindustani parrot had only feigned death as a way for him to escape confinement.

Ahmad grieved deeply over his loss. One day his cousin Mustafa paid a visit and he immediately lamented his woes to him. Upon hearing his cousin's story, Mustafa criticized Ahmad, "By all that is holy, how could you be so ignorant? The earth is for man to walk and the sky is for birds to fly. You cannot change life, or you bring yourself grief."

Ahmad replied, "My dear cousin, many others keep birds in cages, why cannot I?"

"They ignore natural law out of desire and stupidity," Mustafa replied. "Because others do it, you who know better believe you have the same right. Your desire to possess a beautiful bird has clouded your judgment and caused you grief. May you suffer until you meet life on its terms, not on yours. Don't you know that you can't change life? It is what it is."

Sometime later the Baghdad parrot found his way back to brethren in India. He told them, "I truly don't understand men; they are not like us for we only seek food, shelter, and a comfortable environment. While man seeks these things as well, he also tries to change the nature of things, a horrible crime. And they justify this with all manner of excuses, instead of living in harmony with the plentitude of Allah's gifts. In meeting life's challenges, they simply ignore the way life greets them."[1]

Through the ages, sages have told us we are both fully human, creatures of the earth; and we are fully divine, creatures of the sky. We cannot embrace our divinity unless we totally acknowledge and accept our humanness. This requires us to be rigorously honest with ourselves and see the world clearly. If we wear rose-colored glasses and don't acknowledge reality as it is, then our journey through life becomes immensely difficult. When we accept our humanness and the limitations of this concrete reality, we tap our inner wisdom and open ourselves to spirit. The parrots in our story are correct; we need to face life as it greets us or as it is, and not as we would like it to be. As with Ahmed, our desires and our beliefs can act as filters to distort our perception of reality and impair our ability to meet life as it happens.

The Eye of the Beholder

The eye of the beholder sees the world. Some would say it is actually created by our perception of it. When different people look at an elephant, overweight people see its size; people with big noses or ears see those features. The elephant exists independent of our perception, but our subjective orientation determines what we perceive or don't notice. This may be of no consequence on an outing to the circus, but if we're just as subjective in choosing our business partners, spouses and friends, or our stock portfolio, it can greatly impact our lives. I'm not suggesting we root out our personal

---

[1] E.H. Whinfield, The Mathnawi, Adapted from *The Merchant and His Parrot* 2004 New Age Books

quirks; they are what make us unique. Just understand what they are and how they influence our choices.

What I've observed during my own perceptual education is that my friends and associates observe the world through a slightly different lens than I do. I may see grey with a hint of white, while others see grey with a hint of blue or purple. Upon reflection I realize that my perceptual palate of colors is slightly different from everybody else. It is tinted by my beliefs, emotions, and psychological orientation. No palate is the same. We all perceive life differently. To live in harmony with an unpredictable, ever-changing, and often hostile environment, we need to perceive the world with more objectivity, always gauging our subjective orientation. How we interpret what we perceive is vital to our well-being and survival.

As a clinical psychotherapist, I consistently find that my patients' most troubling problem is reacting to the phenomenal world with distorted perceptions. When their interactions with other people and life situations are colored by strong emotions and/or rigid beliefs, they constantly misread what is "out there," locking them into cycles of grief and pain. This is not a new problem. It was part of the human condition since time immemorial. The fact is that the mind and its perceptual faculty have not changed significantly since we first defined ourselves as a species, especially since humans gathered together into social units.

In more ancient times, these concerns were the province of sages and philosophers. Two thousand years ago Patanjali, author of the *Yoga Sutras*, attributed man's suffering chiefly to distorted perceptions. Centuries later the Buddha discovered much the same through his own life experience. Both sages taught that what we call reality is created in the mind and projected on to the world. We all experience different realities because of our varying histories and orientations. This doesn't mean that we disagree that a tree is a tree or a horse is a horse. We don't create the objects in the world, but our reaction to them, filtered through our individual palate of emotions and beliefs, invests them with personal meaning from which we create our values.

The Timely Accident

As an example, my friend Jack was driving with his girlfriend, traveling about fifteen miles per hour when he made a left-hand turn at an intersection. He later told me that he wasn't paying attention and hit a car coming from the opposite direction. As Jack got out of the car, his girlfriend Theresa began crying. The other driver was extremely angry with him for causing the accident. He calmed down and they exchanged telephone numbers and insurance information. As Jack got back into his car, something occurred to him and a smile crept over his face. The other driver standing nearby became incensed. He yelled at Jack for taking the accident so lightly. They were both lucky that nobody had been injured and that the damage was only minor.

What occurred to Jack was that he had wanted to get rid of his car for over a year but never seemed to find the time to shop for another car. The accident was the stimulus he would need to buy a new car. As it turned out, the minor fender bender was a blessing in disguise. Given his perception of the accident, he was naturally surprised that everyone else was taking it so seriously. However, his girlfriend was very upset with him. From her point of view, they were lucky even at this speed that they both weren't badly injured. Meanwhile, one of the bystanders who had seen the accident said Jack was lucky the other car didn't jump the curb and hit them.

Everyone at the scene agreed that an accident had taken place. However, as Jack looked back on it, their experience of the event varied greatly. Theresa perceived it as a personal affront, that Jack wasn't "taking care" of her and could have injured her worse. The other driver, a rushed businessman, was angry that his expensive car was dinged up because of one more complication in his busy day. One of the bystanders was critical of Jack for being careless and negligent and putting everybody at the bus stop in danger. Notice how everybody involved assessed the accident by how it affected them, and their emotional response was an extension of that perception.

When Jack told me about his accident, it reminded me of a story from the *Surangama Sutra*. The Buddha had admonished his student, Ananda, to be careful not to distort his perception of reality. The Buddha said, "Ananda, you do not seem to realize that the sound of the gong, the hearing of the sound, and the perception are three different things, for you replied without recognizing the difference."

The Buddha urged his student to be clear in his mind, to make a distinction between the event that occurred and his perception of it. He emphasized that the event and one's perception of that event are not the same.

The accident illustrates how our emotions, beliefs, and personal concerns determine how we react when something happens to us and we create our own personal reality. With this being the case, it is important for us to step back from our prejudiced perception and assess it more objectively by putting ourselves in the other person's shoes. If Jack had considered that through his inability to resolve issues before they "exploded on the scene," he may have greatly injured

Theresa or even the pregnant woman at the bus stop; he would probably see the accident differently and be less concerned about getting a new car.

The key to living successfully is to take back the projection of your beliefs and the emotions that cloud your perception of reality. You can then act according to how life is rather than how you would like it to be. As Mustafa said to his cousin, you can't change reality; it will keep coming at you forcing your adjustment. This doesn't guarantee that you will always get the result you want, because you don't control the outcome of your actions. You simply enhance your prospects by aligning your desire with realistic expectations, being satisfied with what you need and not what your ego or the hungry child in you wants. Clearly this is not an easy task, and it has been the subject of inquiry for ages.

Elephantine Beliefs

A long time ago in India, a spiritual seeker studied with a renowned spiritual master. This student was very dedicated and diligent in his studies. He was faithful in his spiritual practices and carried them out as taught by his guru. At one point in his studies, he was taught that his soul and the soul of the Lord were one and the same. He practiced a mantra— Tat Vam As—which translates, "I am one with you." He repeated this mantra often. He was also taught that all of creation was permeated with the consciousness of the Lord. Everywhere he went he tried to see the Lord in his manifested world.

One day he was crossing a road and an elephant was approaching. People began shouting at him to watch out for the elephant. He ignored their cries and continued to place himself in harm's way. Finally, the mahout riding on top of the elephant pleaded with him to move out of the way. The sadu (a wandering holy man, or wandering renunciate) calmly clung to his belief. Since the Lord was in every aspect of creation, he was the elephant, too, and it would not injure him. Ignoring everyone's pleas, he stepped into the elephant's path and was badly injured.

As the people pulled his mangled body to the roadside, his guru appeared in the crowd and asked him why he did such a foolish thing. The sadu replied, "God is the elephant, just as you taught me." His guru shook his head and replied, "Yes this is true. But God is also the people and the mahout warning you to avoid the danger of the elephant."[2]

A religious belief that is true on the abstract level doesn't necessarily translate to the reality of the everyday world, and in the end is no different from a psychotic's belief that he can fly and then jumps to his death. As with the sadu, when our entrenched beliefs color our understanding of reality and prevent us from seeing a bigger picture, we usually pay a price. I like to think of the elephant in this story as a metaphor for beliefs that are so large they sometimes blind us to what is happening in the here and now. While the story may appear silly it actually describes a commonplace behavior where our fixed ideas, despite repeated feedback, cause us to ignore reality and its demands.

Getting Unstuck in Our Heads

Life would be so much easier if we could only trust our perceptions 100 percent of the time. As the Buddha's

---

[2] Shri Ramakrishna. *Tales and Parables*. Shri Ramakrishna Math, Chennai

teachings point out, this is not possible. Even so, we all tend to defend our perceptions as right, a phenomenon that is sometimes called being "caught in our heads". I had always assumed that the more educated or intelligent we are the less prone we might be to getting caught in our heads, but that is not the case. As Patanjali said in the *Yoga Sutras*, "The conscious mind can comprehend almost anything, but it is colored by the perception of the seer and the seen..."

No matter how intelligent or insightful, we need to realize that our understanding of events is colored by our personal perceptions. Intelligence alone can't guarantee that we are seeing things clearly, as was the case with the sadu in the previous story. There must be an awareness of the distinction between what is actually happening and what we tell ourselves about it. We need to become aware of our mind's tendency to interpret reality according to its beliefs; we need to take full responsibility for projecting our thoughts onto what is actually taking place *out there*.

Krishna Tests Two Monarchs

One day the Lord Krishna decided to see how two monarchs were governing in his name. He paid an uninvited visit to the court of a king who was cruel, miserly, and mean-spirited. In a blaze of celestial light, Krishna appeared at court and the king humbly bowed before his Lord. He asked the king to travel throughout his kingdom to see if he could find one good person. The king dutifully traveled far and wide across the land and met with a great many people. After several months of searching, the king returned to his throne room and told Krishna that he had done his bidding. The Lord asked him if he had found one good person in his kingdom.

The king answered, "My beloved Lord, I have searched far and wide and talked to all of my people. Although I did find a few who had performed good deeds, most of them were selfish, self-centered, and miserly. I did not find one good person in the sense that you mean."

The Lord Krishna now went to the second kingdom and asked another question of its queen who was known to be fair, kind, and just. He asked her to travel throughout her kingdom to see if she could find one evil person. The queen journeyed to all of her provinces, and after a long and tiresome search, she appeared before Krishna. She said, "Dearest Lord, I have traveled far and wide, and although I spoke to a great many people, some who had done bad deeds, I could not find anyone who was evil."[3]

While this story is ancient, its message is as relevant today as it was ages ago. What we see and the judgments we make are colored by our inner state of mind and being. Or, in other words, we only see what and who we are. Interestingly enough, the above story points out that this can be both an under- and overestimate of the world around us and ourselves. This brings me to another real life example, a woman name Alice who overestimated her son's academic ability and caused both of them a great deal of distress.

Alice in Never-Never Land

Recently Alice and her ten-year-old son Michael visited me. He attended a prestigious private elementary school, and Alice's friends and family raved about its academic reputation. When Michael began to struggle with low grades

---

[3] A Krishna story, source unknown

and behavior problems, they encouraged to keep him in school because of its prestigious standing. The school principal, acting on feedback from Michael's teachers, told Alice that this may not be a good fit for either of them. At our first meeting, I asked if she was placing unrealistic demands on Michael. Since her older son had done well at the academy, Alice had trouble believing that Michael couldn't do the same.

Alice also revealed to me that she had a bias against public schools, believing their curriculum and facilities were inferior to that of private schools. She still believed Michael could benefit from attending the academy despite his recent difficulties. When he continued to do poorly and fell back on his grade average, Alice accused her son of being lazy and not applying himself. This only aggravated the situation; Michael became depressed and soon the situation spiraled downward.

At our next meeting, I told Alice that she needed to assess Michael's situation more objectively; she had to face the fact that as much as she wanted to keep her son in the academy, this wasn't working for either Michael or the school. She had to put aside her bias against public education and seriously consider the local school system as a viable alternative. Alice refused my counsel and applied more pressure on Michael to achieve beyond his ability. He only became more rebellious and his grades dropped even further.

When he became obstinate and insubordinate at home, Alice expected me to "fix" Michael's home behavior and somehow improve his education. I told Alice that her son's behavior was a normal response to unnecessary pressure, and we needed to relieve that pressure. Michael was acting out at home because he was feeling frustrated and inadequate as a result of his inability to perform well at the academy. By confronting her in this way, Alice began to release her strongly held beliefs about the academy being a fit-all situation. She realized that her son might do better in a less "intense" environment. A few weeks later she made a breakthrough.

Alice said to me, "You know, Don, what's important is Michael feeling comfortable wherever he's placed. If that's public school, so be it." She was finally seeing the situation from her son's point of view, not her own. I then told her the elephant story. She laughed and said to me, "I guess I really got stomped on."

One of my favorite ancient texts is *The I Ching*, sometimes called "The Book of Changes," because it teaches about seeing the vacillating face of reality clearly. It was written by Chinese sages during the Shang Dynasty, somewhere between 1600 B.C. and 1027 B.C.[4] It is based on the philosophy of Taoism and Confucianism, and is a fount of wisdom that is as applicable today as it was in antiquity. For example, it tells us that it takes internal strength to look at oneself clearly:

"It is only when we have the courage to face things as they are, without any sort of self-deception or illusion, that a light will develop out of events, by which a path to success may be recognized."[5]

The I Ching repeatedly expresses the idea that it is wise to engage reality with humility and courage. We need to humbly acknowledge the limitations of our internal perceptual realities and leave room for the outside reality to speak to us.

---

[4] I Ching. Ibid

[5] Trungpa, 1973. Cutting through Spiritual Materialism. Shambala Press

When we face life with humility, it will give us valuable feedback. We may experience a visceral sense of correctness about our perception, an "ah hah" moment. Sometimes we may see a ray of understanding that emanates from inside us, or we might feel a sense of relief. These and other wake-up calls issue from the Self, not the ego, and they can be quite clear to the individual. *The I Ching* tells us we must meet the phenomenal world directly to get this kind of feedback.

Sometimes we may approach life with such quietude and humility yet won't receive a "hit," so to speak. *The I Ching* doesn't guarantee us the 'ah hah' moment; it merely positions us to have a good prospect of experiencing one. If we set our ego aside and detach ourselves from perception and still don't get a "hit," we're simply not meant to get one, which is fine. Life will have other messages for us embedded in the choices we make based on our clearest perceptions.

Our beliefs are not the only elephant-sized distortions we might face in clearing our field of vision. We can have elephant-sized emotions as well.

The King Who Desired a Chambermaid

There was a king who was obsessed with sleeping with the queen's chambermaid. He spent much of his time thinking about how he could satisfy his desire without creating havoc. Finally, he thought he could fool his guru into consenting to an illicit affair with a clever argument. One day he said to his teacher that since God is everywhere and in everything, his presence makes everything equal; so sleeping with the chambermaid would be no different from being with his wife. When the queen heard of the king's subterfuge, she immediately went to their guru and asked how they could break the king of this obsession. The saintly man advised her to have patience.

Sometime later the guru returned to the castle for an evening meal with the king and queen. He told the queen, "When you serve dinner this evening, have a pot full of cow dung beside the beef and rice dishes."

The queen did as she was told, and that evening the guru and the royal couple sat down to supper. After the queen and their guest were served plates of rice and beef, the king was presented with rice and cow dung. As he went into a violent rage, the guru quietly told him, "Your Highness, since you are well versed in spirituality, and since God resides in all things, there should be no distinction between the beef and cow dung, as between the queen and her chambermaid."[6]

The King and I

I can't help but think of the numerous humbling experiences I have had when my desire clouded my vision. A couple of years ago, I bought a new pair of cutting-edge skis. I was dying to try them out all season. For many reasons, I wasn't free on weekends that winter. A weekend finally opened up and I couldn't wait to get to the mountains. I watched the weather reports for several days, hoping the storm forecast would somehow change. Rather than change for the better as the weekend approached, the weather report became more ominous. I insisted on going skiing, telling myself that there would be breaks in the storm in the face of obvious warnings that the Sierras were prepared for the worst storm of the season. I set out in the evening from the Bay Area in a blinding rainstorm. I was concerned with the

---

[6] Shri Ramakrishna, Ibid

intensity of the storm but convinced myself that it would blow over and drop in intensity. I could only see myself smoothly navigating the fresh powder with my new skis.

As I reached the mountains, the storm did not let up. By now I should have known better, but I continued to let my obsession cloud my judgment. The snow was virtually blinding and I was only able to travel on the roads at very slow speeds. In spite of this obvious sign, I was fixated by my vision of skiing in the deepest, driest powder of the season. As I drove on, there were makeshift road signs instructing drivers to turn back; cars ahead of me kept turning around and going back down the mountain. Eventually, there were only a few drivers who ignored the signs and ascended the mountain. We'd have the ski slopes to ourselves, I thought. As I navigated a long turn, I saw semi-trailers parked on the side of the road with their drivers wrapped in blankets, sleeping in their seats. This scene did not deter me, so strong was my desire to step into my new skis. Two snowplows blocked the road a few miles ahead. As my ideal skiing trip shattered, a sheriff approached my car and signaled me to stop. I rolled down the window, and he angrily asked why I hadn't heeded the earlier signs to turn back. He said, "It's people like you that cause me to freeze my nuts off in the snow."

I didn't say anything, as I humbly listened to his tirade and turned my car around to head back down the mountain. Approximately ten hours after my departure, I returned to my driveway. My eyes were like tiny red-hot beads from driving in the blinding snow and rain. I was exhausted. Utterly defeated, I dragged myself into bed. I fell asleep muttering to myself, "Dumbo." The emotional elephant blocking my common sense made me pay a dear price. I didn't have the energy to go skiing for the rest of the season, even though we had some spectacularly clear weekends with fresh powdered snow.

Life will give us feedback on our choices. It may not be to our liking but we will get a response. Our emotions and beliefs will always interfere with our ability to discern reality clearly. When we approach life with humility and without an agenda, *we do not risk being right or wrong. Whatever the results, there should be no sense of failure or punishment.* We will experience either success or the lack of it, nothing more. The message, as *The Bhagavad Gita* teaches us, is to act without attachment to the results of action. In the above story, I was so emotionally attached to an image in my mind that I was blinded to the reality of a hazardous situation. Just like the king in our story, I was deluded by my emotions and couldn't see straight, or through the snowstorm.

The *Yoga Sutras* asks us to examine life in all its aspects without prejudice. This is not an easy task and requires discipline. Even with discipline, we are going to make mistakes, but they will be our lessons as well. It is okay to make mistakes. I believe it is important to honor our human nature and not berate ourselves when our emotions and beliefs cause us to make poor choices. On the other hand, it is important to know how we tend to distort what is out there and superimpose our ideas on reality. Awareness is the key.

As I will discuss in the next chapter, life's journey is about personal evolution through the expansion of our awareness. Earlier, I said that reality has its source within us. None of us experiences life the same as the other. I believe this is one of the most exciting realizations we can entertain. *We create our personal reaction to the world; we create our own reality.*

This being the case, you want to be very careful of your creation. The buck stops at your door. Create the best world possible for your development. As a conscious self-reflective human being, you want to expand your knowledge of life and open your consciousness to its penultimate potential. The first step is to objectively read what is *out there* to the best of your ability.

Chapter Two
The Ego's Fear of Self-Created Change

A group of men were watching a game of chess when a sadu walked by and joined them. After a while he told the onlookers, "Your comments about the board moves are more astute than the players because you are not attached to the match."

One of the men asked the sadu, "Dear sir, I thought you didn't bother with trivial matters such as a chess game?"

The sadu replied, "Life is like the board game, always changing, but because you are attached to making the right move, your emotion interferes with your ability to make good choices at the crossroads you face. Try to be an onlooker, and consider the vicissitudes of life as if you were observing a game of chess. You will see things in their true light and can accept them better than other men of the world."[1]

---

[1] *Sayings of Shri Ramakrishna*, Shri Ramakrishna Math, Chennai

We bring a lot of misery into our lives by clinging to the past rather than accepting the changes that come our way. It has been said that the only constant in life is that everything will change. Nothing stays the same. We all know this, yet we frequently have trouble dealing with the challenges life presents. Sometimes we get stuck moaning and groaning about our sorry fate while new opportunities pass by us. Our children fail to graduate from college, we lose our jobs, mom gets sick, our new boss doesn't like us, the doctor tells us we have angina, or the storm pushes our house two feet off its foundation. Intellectually we know that situations and even the people in our lives will change, but emotionally we are often unprepared to cope with the consequences. We get attached, instead of being onlookers as the sadu entreats us.

More of my patients seek help dealing with the vicissitudes of life than for any other reason. Some tell me that the problem at hand was unexpected or came upon them faster than they had anticipated. Most complain that what is happening to them is unfair, and that they are basically good people who don't deserve misfortune of any kind. Those dealing with the loss of a loved one or a cherished relationship are overwhelmed with grief and regret and can't see a way out. Whatever the challenge, we generally experience what I call a "disconnect." There is a separation between what we know to be a fact of life, that change is inevitable, and our lack of preparedness or inability to accept it.

"We Can't Revive the Past."

From time immemorial, sages have written commentaries on this human tendency to resist change. From ancient China comes the wisdom that we are all part of the ever-changing

Tao, or *all that is*, that life flows like a river, moving and changing everything in its course. Confucius is reported to have said, "Everything flows on and on like this river, without pause, day and night . . . He who has perceived the meaning of change fixes his attention no longer on transitory individual things but on the immutable, eternal law at work in all change. This law is the Tao."[2]

The I Ching states the universal law of nature: that the river of time flows continuously, bringing constant change in its wake. Lao-tzu, the 1st century Chinese sage, said of the Tao, "Meet it and you will not see its head. Follow it and you will not see its back." The law is clear. Accept the flow and rhythm of change, and you avoid getting caught in one of life's snares.

This brings to mind a contemporary story from India, the land of ancient wisdom. Within a year of the establishment of modern India, while the country was still in shock after the assassination of Mahatma Gandhi, his followers were perplexed on how to carry forward their leader's reform movement. One could say they were overwhelmed by their grief.

His aides met hoping to convince a close associate of Gandhi, Vinoba Bhave, to carry on with the mission. Along with Gandhi and many others, he had frequently been jailed for civil disobedience before the movement succeeded in breaking the British rule, and he was held in great esteem amongst his peers.

Unwilling to step into Gandhi's shoes, Bhave vehemently

---

[2] Whilem/Baynes *The I Ching*. Bolinger Series XIX, Princeton Press 1985

declined to carry out the reform movement that was the earmark of Gandhi's political platform. He kept repeating to his colleagues, "We can't revive the past. We can't revive the past."

Finally, in memory of his beloved teacher, he agreed to see what effort he could make in carrying out Gandhi's grand scheme. He launched the program Kanchan-Mukti (freedom from dependence on gold, i.e., money) and Rishi-Kheti (cultivation without the use of bullocks, as was practiced by Rishis since ancient times).

In 1951, Bhave started a peace trek on foot in the region of Tlangana where struggles still persisted. There he listened to the complaints of the villagers who had little food. At each small village, the report was the same. "We have no food." He asked them why they didn't grow their own food, and he was told that they were untouchables and therefore didn't own land. Bhave thought about talking to the government in New Delhi about their plight, but realized the government wouldn't help the villagers with this crisis. Even if he got a land grant passed, it would be years before it reached the outlying villages. He told the local villagers they would have to help themselves.

One landowner, moved by the plight of the poor and inspired by Gandhi's ideals, donated eighty acres to the villagers to grow food. As Bhave went from village to village, the word spread and other landowners offered parcels for the lowest castes to work. He continued his land crusade and by the time he returned to Gandhi's council, he had acquired 2200 acres of land for the poorest of the poor. Inspired by his feat, a great many people of goodwill joined in and started the great Indian Land Reform Movement. Ultimately, these men collected ten million acres for the hungry and poor villagers over a fourteen-year period. This had not been a goal of his peace trek, so Bhave didn't "revive the past." He instead created a new future for a great many starving people. He stepped into the river of change and let it move him forward.

The wisdom literature of the ages is replete with stories of change and the impermanence of life. The story of Uttam is one of my favorites because of its humor and insight into the human condition.

The Kingdom Where Everything Worked Out for the Best

Uttam understood the Tao. He had great trust in the law of change. His every utterance at the prospect of change was, "It is God's will." He understood the futility of arguing with life or trying to swim upstream against the flow of the Tao.

Uttam was a devoted minister, friend, and confidant to a righteous king by the name of Chandrasena, who governed his subjects with the gentle and loving kindness of a father toward his children. He reigned over the Kingdom of Patalipurta, and he depended a great deal on the counsel of Uttam. No matter what happened in the functioning of the government or occurred in the personal lives of the king and his family, Uttam always said, "God performs all works for the best. It is God's will."

Occasionally, when affairs of state would go very wrong and the worst results came to pass, Uttam would say, "Don't worry, it's for the best. God has a plan, and He designs all for the best possible results."

This advice would often irritate King Chandrasena. He was frequently beset by numerous problems: enemies of the state, finance, spies sowing seeds of dissension, and the potential of a drought. For the supreme ruler of a kingdom almost anything and everything can go wrong and at any time.

And then, in the midst of havoc, while trying to deal with all of these difficulties, his chief minister would say, "Don't worry. God does everything for the best. Protect your dharma. Do what is right."

"Do I have to listen to this?" thought the king. "What nonsense this man offers! Again and again we have problems, and he tells me not to worry. It's all God's will! How can I run a kingdom like that?"

One day the king was eating from a basket of fruit. He selected a juicy red apple from the basket, and taking a knife he began to peel it. After a moment, his knife slipped and the king cut himself.

"Ouch!" he shouted. He licked his thumb where a slight trace of blood began to appear. "That hurt!" cried the king.

Uttam was sitting on his customary cushion next to the king. Seeing what had happened, he calmly replied, "Don't worry, it's all right. God has a plan. Everything is for the best."

"What do you mean it's for the best?!" the king replied peevishly. "It's my finger that's bleeding! How can this be for the best? What good can come from the king cutting his finger? Guards, throw this idiot in the dungeon!" Immediately they arrested the minister and took him away.

As it would happen, King Chandrasena was very fond of hunting. He would head out most afternoons with his friend Uttam to shoot game in the forest, enjoy the freshness of the outdoors, and seek a brief respite from the pressures of running the kingdom. After this incident, Chandrasena was feeling reckless and went off into the forest by himself without his entourage, which was very dangerous. He started to shoot at deer passing by him, but because of his lack of concentration was unable to hit one.

Just then, a giant wild boar ran across his path. The king pursued the boar on horseback, following him deep into the dense forest. The boar took him on a merry chase for hours, darting in and out of the undergrowth with deceitful maneuvering. After a while, the king had entered a forest bordering on another kingdom. Soon he was hopelessly lost. Then suddenly a band of hostile natives surrounded King Chandrasena. Brandishing their weapons, they commanded this intruder to dismount from his horse.

The king got down from his horse, surrendered his arms, and was taken a captive. The warriors brought this prisoner to their High Priest.

"Ah!" the priest exclaimed, "An excellent offering for sacrifice! Wash and feed him. Tonight we will kill this nobleman, and the Goddess of Death will be pleased with us!" The king tried to protest, but they could not understand his strange dialect and silenced him. He, however, could understand theirs, and he was frightened for his life.

King Chandrasena was led away, and then bathed, dressed in the finest cloth, fed a scrumptious meal, and later bound to the sacrificial post. The priest began to recite his prayers, walking around the post and anointing their offering, first on the forehead, and then the eyes and mouth. The members of the tribe circled the post chanting in bloodthirsty ecstasy. The executioner raised his sword, ready to cut off the king's head.

"Stop!" said the High Priest, as he began to anoint the king's hands. "What is that on his thumb?"

The executioner leaned closer. "It's a cut," he said in disgust, as he lowered his sword.

"This man is not whole," the High Priest proclaimed to all. "He cannot be sacrificed. Our Goddess will not accept him. Release him unharmed as is the custom."

Chandrasena was freed and headed back through the woods to his kingdom, where he soon met up with his advance guard scouring the forest for their king. When he told them what had happened, the soldiers wanted to hunt down these scoundrels and kill them all. "No," the king said, "they have taught me a valuable lesson."

After returning to his palace and after taking some refreshment and needed rest, he summoned his minister, Uttam. "Bring the minister to me," the king told his head guard.

When the minister was brought before the king, Chandrasena related what had happened to him during his adventure in the forest. He told Uttam, "Perhaps what you said is correct, that God works out everything for the best. Surely the cut on my thumb saved me from being sacrificed by the natives in the forest. But here is my argument, how was it for the best that you spent the day in the dungeon?" The king sat back on his throne and smugly awaited Uttam's reply.

Uttam did not hesitate. "Your highness," he said, "I always accompany you on your hunting expeditions. On this particular day, when you were captured by the natives and nearly sacrificed to their goddess, you were saved by the cut on your finger. Well, I was without a blemish, and if I had accompanied you into the forest, it was I who would've been sacrificed! So you see, your Highness, God did work everything out for the best. He has a plan for all that will bring all of us to the ultimate realization of our dharma."[3]

---

[3] Satyananda Saraswati, Swami. Shree Ma. *Kasyapa Sutra.* Devi Mandir Pub. Dehli.1995

A moment of reflection reminds us that misery doesn't simply drop out of the sky. We often experience unhappiness after an event or change in life occurs. However, it is the interpretation we place on the event that impregnates it with personal meaning. Many factors influence this meaning, such as how we handled change in the past, our beliefs about sudden challenges, the behavior we learned from family dynamics, and the influence of the media and other innumerable sources. But the interpretation we place on a situation may have little to no relationship to the reality of the challenge at hand.

As with Jack's incident in Chapter One, an accident is an accident, an illness is an illness, and a job loss is a job loss. It's how we react that creates meaning. Imagine for a moment if following a job layoff, someone said, "Thank God, I'm out of that sweat shop." Rather than see the loss as terrible, the person would be happy to leave an oppressive job, much like how Jack saw the brighter side of his auto accident. One of Carl Jung's biographers tells the story of how a friend had come to Jung depressed after losing his job. Jung said, "Cheer up. Now all of your possibilities are before you."

It is only natural that the first thought we have when encountering perceived negative change is that it wasn't supposed to happen. Bad things aren't supposed to happen to good people, to paraphrase Rabbi Kushner's book title. But, if we reflect upon it, we realize that it is naive to believe that challenges won't occur in the course of our life. Even saints get cancer and die. We are reminded from the bible of the tribulations that "flesh is err to." At such times, we need to revisit the quote from *The I Ching* that reminds us, "Everything flows on and on like this river, without pause day and night."

When we resist change, we lose touch with the ebb and flow of life and need to be reminded that our task is to navigate the shallows and depths of life's currents with humility and respect. Change ushers in an opportunity to reconnect with life the way it is, rather than the way we would like it. It gives us the opportunity to become larger than our histories; to grow and master the change at hand and become better for it. It shows us that all challenges contain the seeds of growth, no matter how life chooses to greet us.

> A man is born gentle and weak.
> At his death he is hard and stiff.
> Green plants are tender and filled with sap.
> At their death they are withered and dry.
>
> Therefore, the still and unbending are the disciples of death.
> The gentle and yielding are the disciples of life;
> Thus, an army without flexibility never wins a battle.
> A tree that is unbending is easily broken.
>
> The hard and strong will fall.
> The soft and weak will overcome.[4]

Uttam was a wise minister who embraced the verisimilitudes of life. He understood that the future doesn't have to be feared. His message was one of trust in God, trust that even unwelcome, frightening change can lead to a good outcome for us and our loved ones. The following story illustrates how Mary didn't let one bad decision prevent her from moving on with her life and finding happiness. Like

---

[4] *Tao Te Ching*

Bhave, she jumped back into the river and caught a bigger fish.

The Honeymoon from Hell

Mary first visited me three weeks after her honeymoon. She told me it had been a disaster. She was in her late twenties and worked in information technology. She met her husband Jacob at work, where he was a rising young star. Mary told me she wanted to marry and start a family and that Jacob had qualities she prized. He was serious, confident, a good provider, and above all he was stable.

She explained that her previous relationships were with less than mature men, and that her family was pressuring her for some time to settle down and start a family. Her parents were thrilled with her *catch*, as they put it, and they adored Jacob. They thought Mary was flighty, and they trusted Jacob to help his wife-to-be to mature. Mary wanted to please her parents, but she also genuinely wanted to settle down and start a family.

She and Jacob had known each other for about six months when they decided to get married. Mary said he was a little controlling, but she thought that he would loosen up when they were married. On their honeymoon in California, Jacob had invited her parents, who were on the West Coast for other matters, to visit them at their wine country retreat. Mary was wary about them visiting at such a delicate time, but she acquiesced to Jacob's wishes.

When they arrived at their honeymoon suite, Jacob informed his new wife that he couldn't stay the whole five days because of business commitments and that he was cutting their honeymoon short. Mary was quite upset but went along with him to keep the peace. On the first night,

Jacob got so drunk that he passed out on the sofa, leaving Mary to talk with her parents long into the night. As they were leaving, her parents again told her how lucky she was to land such a good catch. They advised Mary to just be patient and everything would turn out fine.

The next morning a slightly abashed Jacob brought her parents flowers, and they all sat down together for breakfast in the dining room of the inn. As the conversation flowed, Mary found herself in disagreement with Jacob's ideas about their future as a couple. Her parents chided their daughter for her obstinacy and sided with her husband. Before long, the conversation had turned to Mary's faults and their fears that her childish attitudes would destroy this marriage. She felt that they were ganging up on her, and her rebuttals were drowned out by this onslaught.

Mary ran from the restaurant back to her cabin with Jacob close at her heels. What followed was a big fight. When the yelling and screaming had finally subsided, Jacob told his wife of two days that he wished they had never gotten married. The next day more fighting ensued, and they were unable to bring the weekend's conflicts to an amicable close. When they returned from their honeymoon, they tried couples' counseling, but it didn't help. They both realized it was a hasty decision to get married, and neither party wanted to put in the effort to make the marriage work.

Several weeks after their marriage, Mary told me, "Don, I'm totally fed up with it and want to get out of this awful marriage." I counseled Mary through the divorce. Once the decision was made, it was less painful for her and she was generally relieved to be done with it. There were no children or shared assets at this point, and so it was fairly easy to dissolve the marriage and let both parties go their separate ways.

Afterward I didn't see Mary for nearly six months, and then she called me for an appointment one day. This time Mary came in looking bright and sounding very happy.

"Don, I just told myself to hell with my parents' values and their choices for me. I met a dedicated schoolteacher who doesn't make a lot of money but we have real fun together. My parents don't like him very much, which suggests that I am placing more emphasis on my values than theirs." I had to agree with her.

I was impressed by how Mary was able to deal with her challenge and move on. She corrected this mistake before it became worse and she was saddled with a loveless marriage based on her parents' choices. In the words of the *Tao Te Ching*, she showed herself to be a gentle and yielding disciple of life. Her flexibility enabled her to move forward with her life and created new vistas of opportunity for her.

Mary negotiated her transition successfully. Her story demonstrates that we can manage the difficult events in our lives, experience sadness, grief, and disappointment, yet move on to a new and promising future. She avoided two pitfalls that usually hook most of us into our problems. *First, she didn't hold on to the past.* Her dream of being happily married was shattered with all that it meant to her and her parents, yet she didn't wallow in prolonged remorse. *Secondly, she didn't fear the future* without a mate at her side; she plunged forward, believing the future would offer her opportunities for exploring life.

Clearly we don't want to cut off our emotions, but we can confront our pain and allow it to heal. The greatest impediment to emotional healing is either to deny our hurt or to hold on to it. Our emotions move on just like our thoughts in meditation or clouds in the sky. Unless we consciously or unconsciously choose to hold on to our grief, it too will pass. Everything passes when we let it go.

The other thought that causes us to stay stuck is a fear of the unknown. We don't know what is around the corner, and we fear encountering the future without a roadmap. Imagine for a moment that you are experiencing a difficult challenge and are magically able to fast-forward your life three years along and see yourself enjoying a more fulfilling life. You would be eager to move on and get into your new life. Your thoughts about the future would be positive and you would want to push forward.

Uttam, the king's minister, had a basic trust about life. He knew that life need not be a succession of misery following more misery. He understood that life changed, but trusted that those changes would bring something better. The key for Uttam and us is that we can control our reaction to what occurs, and that makes the unfortunate tolerable, and the good better. The Tao has its bends and curves, and then straightens out for a while. The thoughts we entertain produce fear. Why not entertain thoughts of the good things awaiting us just around the corner, not the bad? We control our reaction to events, and we control our fate to a certain extent.

Nachum's Chest of Sand

There is a famous Mishnaic sage in the Talmud named Nachum Ish-Gamzu. A story is told that the Jews wanted to send a gift to the court of Caesar, and the pious Nachum was sent off with a chest filled with gems and precious jewels. When he was sleeping on the roadside, robbers came and emptied the chest of its precious gems and filled it with sand.

The next day Nachum continued on his trek. He traveled for several days, and one evening decided to look at the treasure he was bringing to Caesar. Expecting to see a chest full of gems, he caught his breath when he saw nothing but sand. Puzzled for a moment, he soon realized that robbers must have made off with the treasure while he was sleeping.

As he gazed at the sand, he uttered his famous line, "Gam zu l'tovah—this too is for the good." And he carried on with his mission. A number of equally disastrous calamities occurred while on his epic journey, and each time he replied, "This too is for the good."

Eventually he reached the court of the Roman emperor and laid the chest of sand before Caesar. As the emperor stared at this offering in puzzlement, a magician came over and revealed that the sand had magical properties.

Caesar was overjoyed with his unusual gift and sent Nachum on his way with a chest filled with jewels and gold, bestowing on him a great honor. Nachum responded on his way out of the palace, "This too is for the best."[5]

Nachum's fortitude stands out in this story. He was besieged by a number of calamities yet saw a deeper meaning (or *fatum*, what the ancients called destiny) in life's vicissitudes. As with Bhave, he wasn't deterred by setbacks and allowed improbable solutions to save the day. When faced with a fearful change, we frequently forget that the threads of our personal salvation are often woven into the rough fabric of change. Hazrat Inayat Khan once said, "When you crush a thorn and grind it, it will turn into a rose

---

[5] Morinis, Alan. *Everyday Holiness* P.72 Trumpeter Press. Boston 2007

for the thorn belongs to the rose. People may not know it, but they are thorns, and when they are crushed the rose comes out of them."[6]

Jackie's Fears in a New Relationship

Jackie was divorced for many years. When I began to counsel her, she had just started a new relationship with a man she met at church. She said she was proceeding very cautiously, not wanting to, in her words, "blow a good thing."

I asked her, "Jackie, what do you mean by blowing a good thing? You said that both of you get along very well, that he's sensitive and considerate, and you are both enjoying yourselves. What is there to blow?"

She said, "Well, we haven't had sex yet, and I know he would like to, but I'm afraid he'll leave me afterwards."

"Whatever gave you that idea?" I asked. "You're enjoying yourselves, are both serious about one another, and he's very caring. If you're not ready to be intimate that's one thing, but if you would like to then what gets blown?"

"Well, it's just that it's going so good I don't want sex to change that."

"Why would it?"

"Don, ten years ago I had a marriage that lasted about eighteen months. After about six or seven months, it started to deteriorate. I began to think that all he wanted was sex. Gradually we drifted apart and I was deeply hurt. You keep telling me that things change and not to get complacent with my life. I just don't want to repeat the same mistake."

---

[6] Khan, Inayat Hazrat. *The Art of Becoming*. P.74 Omega Press, New Lebanon. NY 1989

"Jackie, this relationship is significantly different from your marriage. From what you've told me, all signs indicate that your new guy is more sensitive and caring. Both of you are older. Both of you have said you want to be serious in this relationship. I would be completely surprised if all he's interested in is sex. But, you don't know unless you take a chance; accept that change in this case will be good."

"I know you're right, but I'm afraid."

"Jackie, you didn't know your husband well when you jumped into bed before you were ready. Then you found out that he was insensitive and verbally abusive. This time you've been dating for a while and seem to know this guy much better than your husband at that point. And you're different, more mature, with other values. Don't be afraid of the change, even change within a stable relationship, especially one that has all the earmarks of being important and significant for you. Accept the mystery of what has not yet revealed itself to you. If you're ready to be intimate because your heart is open, don't let fear stop you.

"My experience has been that couples begin to create distance from one another when they don't solve their conflicts and then their intimacy falls off. If your husband was abusive, then a part of you began to pull away long before the marriage was declared over. Probably both of you became dissatisfied with one another. The sexual difficulties were the result of an immature relationship not working, not the other way around. Check it out. Can you remember how you felt about him after the first eight or nine months when the honeymoon ended? Sex changes in a relationship because our feelings change. As long as you work out your current challenges, your love for Raymond will grow and intimacy should follow."

Jackie replied, "The truth is I didn't like the way Bill behaved once we got to know one another better, but I was young and thought my love might change him. It didn't, things got worse, and we hardly spoke to one another. This relationship feels solid; we talk about everything. He has met my family and they get along well. I needed to have someone tell me that change shouldn't be feared. If it's good, things will only change for the better."

Jackie stayed in touch with me for a period of time. In her words, she wanted help "to keep her head on straight." Her relationship continued to develop, and Jackie and Raymond eventually got married. She came back for a "refresher" at that point, since this was a really big change at her age. She was scared, but as she discovered about her intimacy struggle, marriage only made it better.

Jackie found a "good change" scary but eventually rewarding. Jack learned something about himself from a car accident. We need to be aware of the immediate interpretation we put on our changing fortunes, which can be driven by fear from our past. Our job is to flow with change and let the seeds of change unfold in our life. It will often happen despite our resistance. Like Uttam we must learn to trust in providence, and believe that everything will work for the best.

Fire Walking to Heaven

I have meditated for years under the direction of my guru, Shri Anandi Ma. Through her wisdom and the spiritual practices she has bestowed on me, I have gradually learned to accept the vicissitudes of life in a manner which I would never have thought possible a few years ago. In the advice of the sages quoted here, I can hear her voice directing me through the sometimes dangerous shoals of my life experience. My experience in both the psychological and spiritual realms has often helped me more readily understand and apply that advice. It is one of the reasons I find myself writing this book and sharing what I've learned from both disciplines. As is often the case, the same wisdom told from two different perspectives often has a better chance to work on our minds and hearts during times of intense transitions.

Psychology has traditionally concerned itself with integrating our human experience of: emotions, thoughts, images, impulses, and to a certain extent our bodily sensations. It has never made a true distinction between the content of awareness, as in the above list, and awareness itself. It stops short of answering questions about our awareness such as, "who is the perceiver: the person living my life, or the part of me observing him?" The perennial wisdom as spoken by sages throughout the ages approaches such questions by positing that both are true, depending on our focus or level of consciousness. This can instill a certain detachment from experience, but one hard to attain if we're still bogged down with our ongoing emotional issues.

A simple example from my life clearly illustrates the need for both disciplines. When I was in graduate school, I expanded my awareness through meditation, as well as self-hypnosis. But I was particularly troubled by a gnawing anxiety that constantly bothered me. I had anxious dreams. I awoke in the morning and was anxious. I was anxious in school and I rarely had a day when I was free from this anxiety. Then a classmate of mine told me about a fire walk and suggested this might help with my anxiety attacks.

I immediately signed up for it. I knew how to alter my consciousness and knew that I could walk across a bed of hot coals in such a state, despite any anxious thoughts to the contrary. I remembered thinking to myself, "when I cross that bed of coals, I will prove to my mind that I don't have to worry anymore. All my anxiety will be gone." I was truly excited about the fire walk and this prospect. That evening the instructor gradually prepared our group for the event. Prior to the walk, we all held hands in a circle around the bed of coals at about 600 degrees; the heat actually seared the hair off my chest. The instructor went first and I eagerly followed next. It felt as if I was walking on dry ashes across the ten-foot bed of coals. When I landed on the lawn, my feet were cool to the touch.

I felt invigorated, not once had an anxious thought crossed my mind. I had conquered my fears. That night I stayed in town with my parents. In the morning, I woke up with a full-fledged anxiety attack! I was mystified and, absolutely dumfounded. The fire walk of the previous night seemed so distant to me, another life of another person. It felt as if these were two totally different people, the firewalker and me. What I only began to understand later was that I had done the fire walk in an altered state of consciousness, but the next morning my anxiety was occurring in my ordinary waking state. They were indeed two different people, and the challenge was to integrate both levels of consciousness.

In our ordinary walking consciousness, our fearful thoughts and feelings prevent us from accepting many of the basic facts of life, like the fact that life is transitory, that we are born, we live our lives, and we die..., all of us. In deep meditation we can quiet the mind and these anxious thoughts, but even if we label them as just "thinking," it doesn't obviate the fact that our bodies are growing older every minute of every day. But, by facing those fears and accepting that fact as part of the flow of life, and then identifying with that observing, non-changing part of us, we can combine both perspectives, both truths. The encouraging news is that the more we experience deeper states of consciousness and the feelings of peace, joy, love, and oneness that emanate from our soul, the less concerned we are with death. We can then more fully accept the advice of *The I Ching* as it becomes a part of our lives.

"Everything flows on and on like this river, without pause, day and night. . . . He who has perceived the meaning of change fixes his attention no longer on transitory individual things but on the immutable, eternal law at work in all change. This law is the Tao."[7]

---

[7] *The I Ching* Ibid.

Chapter Three
The Infinite Potential of the Self

A long time ago in ancient India, Indra traveled with an Asura (a power-seeking deity) to the home of Brhaspati, the Guru of the Gods. They asked, "Guruji, what is the nature of the Self?" The Guru of the Gods said, "Look at your reflection in the water. What you see is the Self." They both went and looked in the waters of the lake and saw their own reflection. They said, "Guruji meant that this body is the Self." Without questioning this perception, the Asura returned to his people and told them that Brhaspati taught him the body is the Self. He said, "This body is divine. Look for divinity by pleasing your body." All the Asuras were delighted that the body was the Self. They set about pleasing the body with every manner of physical pleasures and over time they became known as devils.

Indra started back home to share this new information with his people, but he became puzzled by the contradiction in what he had learned. He thought to himself, "Sometimes the body gets sick. Sometimes the body is happy and sometimes sad. How can God be either happy or sad? This doesn't make sense. I better go back to Guruji and ask him what he meant by this." Indra returned to Brhaspati. He said, "Guruji, please teach me more about the Self. I don't understand how God can be perishable." Guruji said, "Do more meditation and perform spiritual discipline. Then go back to the waters and tell me what you see."

Indra did as he was told. Following the advice of his teacher, he expanded his awareness through spiritual practices and at some point decided it was time to return to the pool and gaze at his reflection. As he looked at his reflection in the waters, Indra saw his somewhat older face but he now understood that the one who looks into the waters is the Self, not its reflection. Indra returned and told the Gods that the reflection can't be the Self because it is always changing. The Seer is the Self, which is always the same and perceives its own reflection.

As a result of this misunderstanding, the Asuras have taught selfishness and tempted man with promises of delight in transitory things. However, Indra and the Gods from the beginning of time have worked to awaken man's consciousness.[1]

Between the conscious and the unconscious,
the mind has put up a swing:
all earth creatures, even the supernovas, sway

---

[1] Purohit, Swami Shre, and W.B. Yeats Ed. 1985. 2nd Ed. London, Faber & Faber

and it never winds down.

Angels, animals, humans, insects by the million,
Also the wheeling sun and moon;
Ages go by, and it goes on.

Everything is swinging: heaven, earth, water, fire,
And the
Secret One slowly growing a body.

Kabir saw the
Truth for fifteen seconds,
and it made him a servant of the God within—for life.[2]

It is this Self that witnesses or observes our mental activity and is the seat of our awareness. It observes the contents of our mind, spilling forth ideas, emotions, urges, and the like. The Self is the seat of our true I-ness. It doesn't move, change, mutate, or shift in any way. It is this elusive central consciousness that Buddhist and Yogic meditative practices reveal. In the Western tradition, we are less familiar with the formal concept of a witnessing Self. Forms of Christian and Muslim prayer and meditative states allow a similar experience. The methodology and the sustained effort to develop the witness are usually missing, at least for the great mass of people. Interestingly enough, the closest analogue in the West may be the Jungian concept of the objective psyche that nurtures a person's development.

---

[2] Bly, Robert *The Kabir Book*. P.11 Beacon Press Boston. 1977

The Girl who didn't want to be Weird

Some people, particularly those who are creative and/or sensitive, have tapped into their Higher Selves without conscious awareness of it. Frequently this can be a disjointed experience, and they need guidance to help them understand their transcendent experiences and how to integrate them into their daily lives. In this regard, the story of Vanessa comes to mind. A few years back, a very sensitive young woman visited me with complaints of depression and anxiety. Vanessa had a successful career in the technology sector but was very critical of herself. She told me she was an oddball, and had frequent but unsatisfying love relationships that rarely lasted a year. Her friends teased her for being different. Vanessa told me in our first session, "I just want to be like them; I hate being an outsider." As we became acquainted over the next several sessions, she kept repeating two themes. The first with variation was the metaphysical, "What am I doing here?" The second was her constant feeling of rejection. We spent time building trust and identifying her issues.

One day she said to me, "Don, I usually don't share this with anyone, but when I'm alone, I like to read books on space-time warps, the origins of the universe, and books of that nature that I hide from my friends."

I said, "Vanessa, you keep asking yourself 'what am I doing here,' and you read books seeking answers to life's deeper questions. You're not weird, but just asking questions that have perplexed mankind for ages. You're on a search for meaning in a culture that denies it. You're different from your friends but it's a good difference, and one that will bring you answers at some point."

"I thought you were going to think I'm weird," Vanessa

said in relief, "and I was really afraid to say anything. But you're telling me it's okay to be this way?"

We talked about her interests, and I told her that she was ahead of her friends, who might one day do the same, but most people just accept things as they are, and so maybe not. I suggested she continue these pursuits and recommended a few metaphysical books that might broaden her perspective and help on her search for personal meaning.

Gradually Vanessa began to accept her differences but worried excessively that she would never develop a stable relationship. She was codependent and needed an intimate relationship to feel complete. Over a period of several months, she began to accept these needs as part of herself and gradually stopped being critical of them. More important she stopped pathologizing herself and viewed her concern about partnership as problematic, if not anxiety producing.

Vanessa began to actively pursue new interests and attended workshops on meditation. She met other young people with the same concerns and pursuits. These friendships were mutually supportive, and she found spending time with her new friends helped ease the ache of not having an intimate relationship. She began to relish the peace experienced in her group and individual meditations, which seeped into her daily life. The biggest differences were embracing her search for meaning, not thinking it was different, and continuing on a path of expanding her consciousness.

Vanessa's weirdness, which she pathologized, was nothing more than the opening of her consciousness. She was delving into her I-ness, and opening to her Self. By seeking the right psychological help, she gained clarity in distinguishing between the needs of her ego and the emergence of her

Selfhood.

Whether we are aware of it or not, we always carry the Self, our I-ness, within us. Its emergence can be problematic, as in Vanessa's case, forcing us to reconcile its needs with those of our ego. Yet the transition can be made with patience and expanded awareness. In fact, we're all a little like the deer in the Kabir poem that roams the woods looking for what it is carrying within itself:

> Musk lies in the musk deer's own nave,
> But roams in forest it to seek,
> Alike, God pervades hear to heart'
> But men of the world don't conceive
> God exists profuse in each place,
> So don't think less here and more there
> Those who say 'He's far, He's far,
> Those who know Him near, He's near.[3]

The Treasure is You

A poor man of good heart found a treasure map one day. The map promised riches beyond the poor man's wildest dreams. The map instructed him to go out such, and such a door where he would find a dome. "Turn your back to that dome and turn your face toward Mecca; release an arrow, and the treasure is hidden where the arrow falls." As the man thought about the map, news of it reached the king. He immediately sent his best archers to the dome and instructed them to follow those precise directions and let their arrows fly, but still no treasure was found. Upset with his archers, the

---

[3] Algan & Helminski. *Rumi's Sun* Morning Light Press. P.11. 2008

king sent word throughout the kingdom for men who were skilled with the bow to come and find the treasure.

The simple man was puzzled by the instructions. He thought to himself, "If the king and all his archers cannot find the treasure, what chance do I have? This map is probably the clever work of a jokester and I have been a fool." Later that night in a dream a voice told him, "You did not follow directions; we did not say to draw the bow." The next day he arose early while the kingdom was still asleep, and returned to the designated spot. He now followed the directions precisely, put an arrow in the bow, but did not draw it. Upon release the arrow fell at his feet. Puzzled, he then heard a quiet voice inside him say, "You are at the goal; it is within you, Plumb the depths of yourself to find what is much greater than gold."[4]

The Ego is Clueless

The Self doesn't easily reveal itself. Divine consciousness emerges slowly as the individual works to uncover the treasure within them. To make the effort more challenging, the ego is clueless. When we are suddenly or unexpectedly confronted with a challenge, our ego immediately reacts to protect us from the difficulties at hand. The ego activates several defense mechanisms automatically, most of which can be counterproductive to working through the problem. It additionally triggers our emotions, clouding our judgment and preventing us from accurately perceiving the situation at hand. These automatic reactions prevent most of us from shifting our level of awareness to access the wisdom of our I-

---

[4] Bly. Ibid. P. 25

ness or God Self, one capable of meeting and resolving any and all challenges. Otherwise the ego will rely on past histories and merely perpetuate the same faulty fixes.

Psychology can help integrate the wisdom of the masters by giving us tools to deal with the ego, its repression, and even our neurosis, which can be used to shield us from the transcendent. Vanessa was depressed and highly anxious when I first met her. With the help of cognitive therapy, she discarded outmoded beliefs about herself and learned to think more critically and accurately about her real needs. She was able to accept her frailties without judging herself inferior. Finally, she was able to pursue her interest in expanding consciousness, meeting similar people and finding a support group for further exploration and development. Without the benefit of Western psychology, these first stirrings of the Self would've been drowned out by conflicting impulses, buried under a mound of depression. And she would've sought relief in a series of unsatisfactory relationships. As Vanessa dis-identified from her ego processes and analyzed them more objectively, she began to heal herself. Her consciousness expanded as she pursued non-temporal interests, allowing her to experience greater peace, joy, and an excitement for life that was heretofore unknown to her. This allowed for an easier transition from self-rejection to discovering that the source of happiness was within her. "Those who know He's near, He's near."[5]

The masters have admonished us to accept the flow of life. The Tao is your teacher. Know that more enrichment awaits you at the next bend in the river. Your own Self beckons you

---

[5] Algan & Helminski, Ibid.

forward into deeper knowledge and wisdom. The source of peace and wisdom is within you. The following story from the *Upanishads* reveals a secret that is several thousand years old.

God Finds a Home

Long before humans kept written records, the following teaching was passed down from storyteller to storyteller. Sages roamed the countryside carrying the perennial wisdom to those eager to hear it.

"God thought: Can they live without Me? How shall I enter the body?" He knew that if the tongue spoke, breath breathed, eyes saw, ears heard, skin touched, and mind thought, they would not know Him.

He opened the suture of the skull, entered through the gate, which is called the Gate of Joy. He found three places in the body where He could live, three conditions where He could move: waking, dreaming, and sleeping.

He entered the body, named its various parts, wondered if there could be anything there not Himself, rejoiced to find there was nothing but Himself.[6]

Indra was confused when his guru told him to look into a pool of water and gaze at his reflection to find an answer to his question. He couldn't understand how God could be perishable. Finally, with further instruction he went to the pool and gazed again; this second time he understood that the person who witnessed the reflection was eternal and not the person performing the exercise.

---

[6] Source unknown

Our Dual Nature

When we observe ourselves thinking, we are both the thinker and the person watching the thinker. With practice we can create distance between these two parts of us and experience our dual nature. As Indra discovered, the witness is the aware part of our self that sees its reflection in the pool of activity. The thinker is the part that makes conclusions about the image. The thinking part may think, "I look tired today." The aware part sees the reflection and observes the thoughts. The more we develop our witness-self, the more we can detach ourselves from the constant stream of thoughts and emotions that pour through us and not react to them. However, we need to integrate both parts to realize our ultimate selves.

Our ego is programmed to help us survive in the green or concrete jungle. As Homo sapiens we have not changed significantly since our species first evolved on planet Earth. Many of our adaptive reactions were primitive and helped us survive incredible hostile environments. We learned to fear the unknown because the unknown environment was dangerous. Hostile tribes, vicious animals, and other life threatening dangers lurked outside our known territory. Today, most of us live in a somewhat civilized environment where the most serious threat to our physical health may be an encounter with a drunk driver. Yet many of us still fear the unknown world beyond our close-knit circle.

If someone threatened to attack our ancestors, they were in grave danger. Their instinctive reaction was to attack first or flee from any threat of violence, the fight or flight syndrome. Today, if we are verbally attacked, the same self-preservation mechanism comes into play and our immediate urge is to strike back with a verbal retort or a right hook; or just walk away, even though the danger is no longer life-threatening.

In primitive times we needed to band together to survive. The tribe protected us. If we left the tribe and faced a harsh environment alone, we placed ourselves in grave danger. Fear caused us to move very carefully through our environment. Today, if we leave the security of a marriage or our support group, the anxiety might cause us grief. Still the threat to our physical survival is not as grave.

When we experience the inner witness, we observe our thoughts and emotions, and find that most of them are conditioned responses to an imaginary environment. If someone insults you, your immediate urge is to counterattack. If you center yourself and call forth the witness within, you can observe your thoughts and emotions as they automatically arise in response to an insult to your ego. As the witness, you are centered in the moment, observing reality as it takes place. You are in the "now," while a part of you is dancing to the tune of your environment. You can observe your ego's self's reaction to the incident, while remaining the observer. In this way you experience your dual nature.

The more you learn to become a witness of your life, the more you can detach from the robotic movements of your ego. This witness state, which Indra called the observing self, eventually allows you to watch your life unfold and choose your reaction to situations rather than let them control you. Ultimately, you reach deeper and deeper into the Self as you watch your life unfold as an observer, like the sadu entreated us. God cannot be found in the past or future, only in the present moment. As you establish yourself in the observing self, you move deeper into the God within.

A stage comes when the seeker finds that the solid world

is really a mental world; that is, we cannot experience anything except through the mind. We still move in and out of the experiences of the "small self," but are able to witness experiences through the prism of the eternal self. As the mind slowly releases its filters, the seeker comes into greater contact with pure consciousness and the material world is accepted and honored for what it is…, a testing ground. The seeker lives in the world and accepts life as it comes, but is generally unperturbed by its vicissitudes, accepting them as part of everyday life on planet earth. We use our mind to deal with secular activities, but even during these activities we sense the presence of God.

"The path that leads to the Truth is one of two possibilities: either it is through the opening up of the inner universe, or through acquiring knowledge through clearing one's inner impurities. Where else but Hell could be the place of those who leave aside both of these two ways?"[7]

When we disregard either path, we fail to experience our divinity. We are experiencing our personal hells like the man in the following story.

"One cold winter night, a young man decided to light a fire to ward off the winter cold. He traveled some distance until he came upon a village. By the time he reached the village, he was near freezing. He knocked on several doors but no one answered. Near the end of town, he saw a light in a house and knocked on the door. A man came to the door and asked him what he wanted. He said he needed a candle to take with him to light a fire. The villager looked at him and said, "Ha, you are a fine man indeed! You took the trouble to come here and do all this door knocking. But, you are

---

[7] Algan & Helminski, Ibid.

carrying a lighted lantern in your hand." What a man seeks is near him. Still he wanders from place to place in search of the Light.[8]

Abandoned by God

Pat was a successful businessman with a stream of investment successes that spanned nearly thirty years. As he dragged himself into my office for an appointment, he told me he was a victim of the dot-com bust. He owned some office buildings that were being vacated, and he was in a panic that he might lose them. His business ventures were at breakeven due to the recession that followed. Pat had been prudent in his investments, averse to risk, and had worked diligently to build a comfortable life for himself. When I first met him a while back, I felt strongly that life was going to teach him that we don't have total control and that at some point we need to turn stewardship of our life over to a higher force than the ego. Now at mid-life, his grasp on affairs was loosening and he was in a crisis.

Pat belonged to a church and had a number of friends amongst the congregation. He was at a loss to understand how his business affairs had suffered because he considered himself a good Christian. His pastor counseled him frequently, but Pat remained in misery, afraid his personal world would collapse. He became so ashamed by this downturn that he withdrew contact with the church and his friends there. He sought out other churches but was unable to fill the emptiness and hopelessness he was experiencing. A

---

[8] Sri Ramakrishna, *Sayings*. P.267 Shri Ramakrishna Math. Chennai. 2003

distant relative called him complaining about her life, and he told me how empathetic he felt toward her. Pat shared some of his own grief over recent losses, which formed a bond between them and allowed him to support and comfort her during this time of travail. I told him that this might hold the meaning of his recent financial problems. He had experienced pain and could now identify with deep pain in others. We discussed how loss can sometimes be a Godsend. It breaks down our defenses, allows deeper aspects of ourselves to come forward, and encourages us to develop other resources. Personally, I felt that Pat would find an outlet for his natural empathy that could be more rewarding than his previous business success.

After a year of therapy, Pat's business ventures had not recovered, and he started experiencing brief panic attacks. The possibility of bankruptcy was a great strain on him, and we agreed that he should reduce his stress level by slowly liquidating his properties. He had trouble selling some assets at a loss and kept telling me that he could've held on if he were younger. Nevertheless, as he cashed out of his business, the strain lessened. Pat sold his house and moved to a new community, where he joined another church whose members didn't know of his recent failure. He sought religious comfort but found it in an unexpected way. The pastor was a young man, recently married, who worried about building a congregation. Pat formed a warm bond with the young couple, and they began to visit him and his wife for Sunday dinners. Pat helped the young pastor with church financial matters. A father-son relationship developed as the minister shared his anxieties and fears; Pat was surprised that he welcomed this intimacy. One day he told me that he no longer felt abandoned by God and that he derived great comfort and peace from helping others. Toward the end of his transition, Pat started a one-man service business where his newfound people skills were an asset. Three years after our first visit, he was finally ready to move on. Occasionally he would drop me a postcard saying that he was very happy and stress free.

Pat's story could be the story of everyman. At midlife other resources deep within us often seek an expression, as they did in this case. The love and support that Pat eventually shared with others couldn't be expressed fully until he let go of his need for success, money, and prestige. As dark and as hopeless as his financial downturn had seemed at the time, he found an enriching and fulfilling life just around the bend. The God or God-Self that had abandoned him had only nudged him to let go of the limiting ideas about himself, his life, his prospects for happiness, and, most importantly, his concept of God. He found that helping others can often be more "profitable" than just helping yourself to another slice of material success. He had learned the centerpiece wisdom of his religion, which is "whatever you do to others, you do unto yourself."

Pat's story is typical of many modern people. His connection with his church was more from childhood prodding and the desire to attend church as a model to his children. He liked the minister and accepted his religion intellectually. But, as he began his life transition, what had sustained him and supported his roles in life were gradually removed. His ego supports continued to slip from his grasp. While in the middle of this transition, he found profound empathy for a relative and deeply identified with her fear and pain. As his heart was touched with compassion, he had a deep experience of satisfaction helping someone else. In doing so he released his worrisome thoughts and was completely present to her. Perhaps, for the first time in his life, he was touched by a selfless love through being totally present for someone else.

This was his first real spiritual experience. After this turnaround, it occurred more frequently. When Pat centered into his loving kindness, he could bring forth gifts for others. Eventually, this constant dipping into the presence revealed a love of God for man coming through him. As time passed, he was able to experience the Presence within and eventually he brought this gift to more and more people, deepening his movement into the personal sacred. Pat moved slowly from an intellectual understanding of God, with all its limitations, to a pure experience of God deep within himself that nourished him and others.

ONE, ONE, ONE
The lamps are different,
But the Light is the same.
So many garish lamps in the dying brain's
Lamp shop,
Forget about them,
Concentrate on essence, concentrate on Light.
In lucid bliss, calmly smoking off its own holy
Fire,
The Light streams toward you from all things,
The lamps are different,
But the light is the same.
One matter, one energy, one Light, one
Light minded
Endlessly emanating all things,
One turning and burning diamond,

One, One, One
Ground yourself, strip yourself down,
To blind loving silence.
Stay there, until you see
You are gazing at the Light
With its own ageless eyes.[9]

---

[9] Algan & Helminski Ibid. P.137

Chapter Four
Princes and Ogres: Integration of Psyche and Soul

My granddaughter Mikayla was playing at the beach one day with a group of children who were running in and out of the ocean. Near the end of the day, they decided to dig a big hole in the sand and fill it with water. They took turns soaking, splashing, and giggling in the mud hole, having great fun but getting filthy. Eventually I told Mikayla that she needed to wash off as we got ready to leave the beach. As we headed toward the showers, she told me that she had already cleaned herself and didn't want to shower. I said washing herself with dirty water didn't count. She insisted that she was clean enough. Finally Mikayla took a shower and changed into fresh clothes. On the drive home, she wanted to know if she could skip her bath that evening having already showered. I laughed, making note of her response. That night before bedtime, she claimed to be the cleanest child alive after taking her customary bath.

At times all of us act like four year olds stuck in the past—

or in the mud, as in Mikayla's case— unable to adapt to new situations, employing old tactics that can no longer solve our current problems. For thousands of years, sages have noted this human tendency to live in the past and deal with the present using outmoded means. This was a problem in slower times. But at today's accelerated pace, we need to move and adapt quicker or get left behind. The renowned mythologist Joseph Campbell tells a classic story of Prince Five-Weapons who found himself in a similar predicament.

Prince Five-Weapons

A young prince had just completed his military studies under a world-renowned teacher. Having received, as a symbol of his distinction, the title Prince Five-Weapons, he graciously accepted with a bow the gift of five weapons from his teacher. Armed with the new weapons, the prince struck out on the road leading back to the palace of his father the king, some distance away. At one point he came to the entrance to a large forest where people on the road warned him. "Sir, do not enter this forest," they said, "an ogre lives here named Sticky Hair, who kills every man who enters his domain." They described the ogre in horrific detail.

But the prince was confident and as fearless as a lion, and he entered the forest just the same. When he reached the heart of it, the ogre showed himself. The ogre had increased his stature to the height of a palm tree, his head as big as a summer house with a bell-shaped pinnacle, eyes as large as alms bowls, two tusks as big as giant bulbs or buds; he had the beak of a hawk and his hands and feet were dark green. But his most striking feature was a thick coat of matted hair that covered his entire body.

"Where are you going?" he demanded. "Halt! You are in

mortal danger. Leave my forest immediately."

Prince Five-Weapons answered without fear, with great confidence in the arts and crafts that he had learned. "Ogre," said he, "I knew what I was about when I entered this forest. You will do well to be careful about attacking me; for with an arrow steeped in poison, I will pierce your flesh and fell you on the spot!"

Having thus threatened the ogre, the young prince fitted his bow with a poisonous arrow and let it fly. It became stuck to the ogre's matted hair. Then he let fly, one after another, fifty arrows. All stuck to the ogre's hair. The ogre shook off the arrows and let them fall at his feet. Prince Five-Weapons threatened the ogre a second time, drawing his sword and delivering a masterly blow. The sword, thirty-three inches long, also stuck to the ogre's hair. Then the prince smote him with a spear that became stuck as well. Seeing that his spear had become stuck, he smote the ogre with his mighty club. That too stuck right to his hair.

Finally, the prince said, "Master Ogre, you have never heard of me before. I am Prince Five-Weapons. When I entered this forest infested by you, I put my trust not in such weapons as bows; when I entered this forest, I put my trust in myself. Now I am going to beat you, pound you into powder and dust!" Having thus made his determination known, with a yell he struck the ogre with his right hand. The hand stuck to the ogre's hair. The prince struck him with his left hand that was also stuck. He struck him with his right foot. That too stuck. He struck him with his left foot. Again it stuck. He next proclaimed, "I will beat you with my head and pound you into powder and dust!" He struck the ogre with his head. That also stuck right to the ogre's hair.

Prince Five-Weapons was snared five times, stuck five

times, and was now out of weapons. As brave and courageous as he was, the young prince had placed himself in quite a predicament. It certainly didn't look as though he would emerge successfully from this trial, did it?

As for the ogre, he thought to himself: This is some lion of a man, no doubt of a noble birth—no mere peasant! For although he has been caught by an ogre like me, he appears neither to tremble nor to quake! In all the time I have harried this road, I have never seen a single man to match him! Why pray, is he not afraid? Not daring to eat him, he asked, "Youth, why are you not afraid? Why are you not terrified with the fear of death?"

"Ogre, why should I be afraid? For in life one's death is absolutely certain. What's more, I have in my belly a thunderbolt for a weapon. If you eat me, you will not be able to digest that weapon. It will tear your insides into tatters and kill you. In that case, we will both perish. That's why I'm unafraid," uttered Prince Five-Weapons. Hearing those words, the ogre gently put the young Prince down with great respect and admiration and allowed him to proceed on his way.[2]

Notice our young prince dangling from the ogre's hair helplessly, appearing to have exhausted all his existing resources. We know his predicament. He represents all of us when we rely on old knee-jerk reactions to deal with present challenges and get stuck in a sticky situation. Just like the prince, we'll use variations of the same approach and actually make things worse with each try, until we draw upon

---

[2]   Joseph Campbell *The Hero With A Thousand Faces* p.85 Bollinger Series. 2nd Ed   Princeton 1973

different resources to defeat our demons. Prince Five-Weapons was at the end of his proverbial rope. But, for all that, he remained unafraid, undaunted. What was the secret of his fearlessness?

After the prince had exhausted the weapons of his ego to solve this problem, he opened a space for his higher self to enter and apply a little crazy wisdom to the situation. How many times have we encountered an intractable life challenge and relied on old tactics that just don't work this time out? In such cases we're like the young prince trying to beat the problem to death, when what is required is a lighter or different approach, usually one that removes our ego from the equation.

Earlier we had drawn on the wisdom of *The I Ching*, "It is only when we have the courage to face things as they are that a light will develop out of events, by which a path to success may be recognized."[3] Or, when we misperceive what we encounter, seeing it as too big or too little, we often employ the wrong tactic to solve the problem. Prince Five-Weapons didn't see the problem the ogre presented. Even after his egotistic confidence wasted fifty arrows and the rest of his arsenal to the hair of the beast, the feeling of invincibility remained; he kept throwing wood on the fire. Ever have that experience?

At such times, we need to acknowledge that we don't completely understand the complexity of the challenges before us. We have to step back and not allow our knee-jerk responses to rule us, honestly seek a wider perspective with

---

[3] Wilhelm, Richard, trans. 1967, *The I Ching*. Princeton, NJ Princeton Univ. Press.

humility and openness. This will expand our awareness, and we will often find that our challenge requires more time and patience than we have previously anticipated. We're always looking for quick fixes. But most life situations are far too "sticky" for that, and if we're listening, we'll get instant feedback. This will also allow deeper parts of us to adjust and bring forth the needed resources to stay the course and resolve the dilemma. Prince Five-Weapons should've realized that his approach wasn't working when his hail of arrows did not slay the ogre. It takes courage to let go and follow our inner advice when ego tactics are ineffective. Continuing only intensifies the problem, as was the case here.

Such Sticky Hair challenges will scare us, and while fear is an emotion vital to our survival, it can cloud our judgment and color our perception. We need to face our fears, accept them, and read the situation more objectively. We can be a witness in regard to our problem, even as we are co-creating it. This allows us to create a larger perspective that begets a more constructive attitude. You may find, as I have, that there are some basic truths that underlie such experiences. I call the first *"no accident truth."* There are no accidents. Everything occurs for a reason. The second truth is that *life has meaning,* that our personal trials and tribulations are meaningful. The third is that *evolution is beckoning us forward,* and our current challenge has elements that can expand our consciousness. Acknowledging these truths allows us to seek the most comprehensive assessment of any challenge we face.

As we shift into a state of expanded awareness, we merely set the stage for a battle royal. The ego state of conditioned thinking with its multitude of emotions will not readily let go. Sometimes our expanded awareness will be dominant, and at other times our ego. When I was troubled by anxiety in graduate school, I signed up for the fire walk knowing that I could alter my state of conscious and prove that "when I crossed that bed of coals all my anxiety will be gone." In this case, I was able to shift out of ego and bring an expanded awareness to bear. Unfortunately, driven by my ego's need for self-justification, I also drove through a blizzard in an attempt to try out my new state-of-the-art skis until the police—who often represent higher authority in dreams— turned me back. In both cases, the "opportunities" were no accidents, the perfect opportunities for learning some of life's lessons, and they both nudged me on my way to greater awareness.

Dive deep, O mind; dive deep in the Ocean of God's
   Beauty
If you descend to the uttermost depths,
There you will find the gem of Love
Dive into the heart's fathomless depths,
Where many a precious gem lies hid.
But never believe the bed of the ocean bare of gems
If in the first few dives you fail;

With firm resolve and self control
Dive deep and make your way to the goddess's realm.[4]

Krishna's Advice

The Bhagavad Gita's spiritual relevance and practical advice are second to none amongst ancient texts in helping us realize

---

[4] *The Gospel of Ramakrishna*, Swami Nikilananda 1952. P.153 Ramakrishna Vivekananda NY

our fullest potential. Krishna, as Lord, advises Arjuna how to awaken the transcendent impulse and break the boundaries of egocentric existence where he can experience spiritual liberation. Krishna tells Arjuna not only how to reach these sublime states of consciousness, but that his existence must also be grounded in daily work. Arjuna learns to not shirk his work, but to embrace it as an offering to the divine.

Two opposing armies are ready to clash when the story of the *Gita* begins. Arjuna, the greatest archer of his time, stands in his chariot with trumpets blazing, banners flying, war drums rumbling, and conch shells and horns blaring. He looks down on the mightiest army he has witnessed and is filled with fear. As he looks closer, Arjuna sees in both armies " . . . fathers, grandfathers, sons, grandsons,; fathers of wives, uncles, masters, brothers, companions, and friends."[5] Overcome with grief he says, "Life goes from my limbs and they sink, and my mouth is seared and dry; a trembling overcomes my body, and my hair shudders in horror. My great bow falls from my hands, and the skin on my flesh is burning: I am no longer able to stand, because my mind is whirling and wandering."[6]

At a symbolic level, Arjuna faces the battle of his soul, which is tossed between the forces of good and evil. He falls to his knees overwhelmed by the fight that lies before him. The opposing army is the *thoughts and ideas* in his mind. They are man's selfishness, anger, lust, thoughtlessness, cruelty, self-absorption, and aggression. He also fights the self-

---

[5] *The Bhagavad Gita*, trans. 1.26,27. Juan Mascaro.1985 Penguin Classics. NY, NY

[6] Ibid.1.30

limiting idea that he is less than capable of winning this battle. Yet he must because it is his dharma and his karma. His lot is our lot; we must engage the forces that battle within us, whether we want to or not.

Krishna, as the Lord or Higher Consciousness ever present in the Self, urges him on, "Arjuna, Think thou of thy duty and do not waver. There is no greater good for a warrior than to fight this war. But to forgo this fight is to fall into transgression . . . Happy are those whose fate it is to fight such war."[7] The message is clear. Without these tumultuous battles to spur us on, we would never reach deep within our psyche and uncover the Self covered over by the ego's fears. The war we must engage is the inner battle between the desire of our senses and the higher states of consciousness residing in the Self. "All is clouded by desire. Wisdom is clouded by desire . . . desire and passion are the enemy of the soul,"[8] Krishna urges us to use our intellect. "Kill therefore with the sword of wisdom the doubt born of ignorance that lies in thy heart."[9]

Personal experience of God and merging with the divine are the goal of the *Gita*. This is accomplished by loving God and seeing God throughout creation, and particularly in our fellow human beings. "Not by the Vedas (ancient spiritual texts), or an austere life, or gifts to the poor, or ritual offerings can I be seen as thou hast seen me. Only by love can man see me, and know me, and come unto me . . .. The Yogi who sees himself in the heart of all beings and he

---

[7] Ibid. 2.31,2
[8] Ibid. 3.39
[9] Ibid. 4.42

sees all beings in his heart . . . then I never leave him and he never leaves me."[10] The love that Krishna speaks of is akin to the spiritual marriage Christian saints experienced. This story reminds me of St. Theresa of Lisieux or Hildegard of Bingen. These experiences of ecstatic union transcend sectarian creeds and religions. When we love God with all our heart and strength, as Jesus admonishes us, the Microcosm (man) and the Macrocosm (God) can be one, and that unity is then expressed throughout creation.

Arjuna asks how one comes to this high yoga and Krishna tells him to fix his mind on God. "With reason armed with resolution let the seeker quietly lead the mind into the Spirit, and let all his thoughts be silent. And when the mind unsteady and restless strays from the Spirit, let him ever and forever lead it again to the Spirit."[11] Krishna stresses that our lives must be a meditation on God and that we are to look for God in every man.

As we touch divine love, we do not escape into our inner sanctum and avoid duty. Rather, the transcendent love is brought forward into our daily lives. Divine love becomes human love, manifesting itself in peace, respect, gentleness, understanding, and friendship for all sentient beings. Love of the planet uplifts all humanity. When we uplift others, we uplift ourselves; when we denigrate others, we denigrate ourselves because the I in us is the same as the I in them. "He sees himself in the heart of all beings, and he sees all beings in his heart. This is the vision of the Yogi of harmony, a vision

---

[10] Ibid. 6.30
[11] Ibid. 6.25,6

which is ever one."[12] We understand that the golden rule Jesus taught, "love our neighbor as ourselves," is founded on a deep metaphysical principle.

Krishna tells us to use our intellect to control the lower functions of the ego. The pleasure principle is very strong and material attachments and pleasures are seldom satiated. We can respect this part of ourselves without falling into debauchery and neglecting the greater riches awaiting our discovery. When we reach inward into a pure potentiality, we are able to face life's challenges. We remind ourselves that the Divine is infinite, and that when we touch the Divine within ourselves, we touch on infinite possibilities. Major challenges require us to do just that—to call upon the resources of the Self, as Prince Five-Weapons did at his moment of truth.

Sticky Hair Challenges

When we face Sticky Hair-type challenges, it is our dharma that has brought these challenges. There is no escape. We may not like the immensity of the challenges, and we may quake in our boots as Arjuna did before his mighty battle, but we must push forward. "If thou wilt not fight thy battle of life because in selfishness thou art afraid of the battle, thy resolution is in vain: *nature will compel thee.*"[13] We must constantly remind ourselves that we are battling our thoughts, emotions, and frailties that are called forth to our awareness. As I've said, our attitude will determine how successfully we meet our challenge. Although they occur in reality—illness, death of a loved one, or business loss—our real battle is on

---

[12] Ibid.6.29
[13] Ibid. 18.59

the inner planes. What is really at stake is our personal evolution, as it was for Arjuna.

We have to struggle against letting the ego evaluate our trials by its faulty definitions. The lower mind can only define problems in terms of its narrow perception. If we don't struggle against this limited perspective, we are like the child in the mud puddle, pouring dirty water over ourselves and thinking we're cleaning ourselves. We need to find the clean, pure water of spirit, which is the province of the witnessing Self. And it is not sufficient to just step into this space, because our ego's thoughts and fears will creep inside as well. We must constantly nurture ourselves with the truths: there are no accidents, everything occurs for a reason, and our current trial contains the seeds for the expansion of our consciousness. We must nurture ourselves with the truth that our basic essence, our I-ness or our Self, is seeking emergence. The God within is waiting. "And when a man sees that the God in himself is the same God in all that is, he hurts not himself by hurting others; he goes indeed to the highest path."[14] This resonates with the words of Jesus, "I am the way, the truth, and the life, no one comes to the Father, but by way of Me."[15]

"The true light that enlightens every man was coming into the world, and the world was made through Him."[16]

I was discussing these ideas with a very good friend of mine. Phil, a strong practicing Catholic, said to me, "Don, you're absolutely right. But every time I turn it over to God,

---

[14] Ibid. 13.28
[15] *Holy Bible*. John 12.6
[16] Ibid. 1.9

every time I let go to God, I take it back, and suffer again."

"You're right, Phil; it's happened to me as well," I told him. "Do you know why you take it back?"

"Sure. After a while, I just get scared. Letting go means losing control."

"Phil, that's the crux of it. The ego wants to control everything, even if it leads to more misery." He nodded his head. "All of us have the problem. The only solution is to cultivate the opening of the Self, deepen our movement into the Self, and then the truth becomes strong enough that it silences those ego fears."

There are many paths to God. We need to follow the one that has our name on it. The path may twist and wind itself through a changing terrain, but we will know it is ours by our intuition, when we are still enough to listen to it. And it is not enough to follow a path that merely has heart for us; we must demand more of ourselves. We must ingrain that path in our heart by living the teaching day in and day out. We must make it a reality for us; instill the truth in our hearts. This takes hard work and dedication. We must roll up our sleeves and do what's required. There is no easy way. Then, when we experience the Sacred every day of our life, the ego's falsehood will loosen its grip on us.

At such a point, Arjuna complains that it is very hard to follow Krishna's advice. "My mind is inconsistent: it is restless, it doesn't find rest . . . it is impetuous, self-willed, and hard to train: to master the mind seems as difficult as to master the mighty winds."[17]

Krishna replies, "Arjuna, the mind is indeed restless. But

---

[17] *The Bhagavad Gita.* 6.34

by constant practice and by freedom from passions the mind in truth can be trained."[18]

My guru, Shri Anandi Ma, stresses that we spend time meditating daily. She tells us not to lose a day without touching the Sacred within us because it is a day lost forever. Daily practice is essential in order to reap the benefits of spiritual work. We are like cloth that is dipped into dye. We need to be dipped constantly to take on the color of the dye. One dunking is not sufficient. When we're constantly immersed in spiritual practice, our self becomes the Self. Then, when we turn it over to God, the voice of the Self drowns out the little voice of the ego. Shri Anandi Ma also teaches that each of us is different. In her words, some of us would want to drive a car from the West Coast to the East Coast, others would take the train, and yet some would fly. Whether our vehicle is the car or the airplane, eventually we all wind up in the same place. Her point is clear. Some of us move faster than others towards self-realization. It's not the speed of movement that is important but that we ride our own vehicle and don't detour because our progress appears slow. Keep the goal in mind, not the vehicle of travel. The Self awaits us.

The Ego's Bad Rap

We have explored how the ego can hold us back from discovering our personal truth. Almost every story and vignette in this book tells how the ego fumbles the challenge at hand. It would thus appear without reflection that the ego is the culprit that keeps us from knowing the truth. This is

---

[18] Ibid.6.35

not always the case. As the Master Carpenter once said, "Give unto Caesar that which is Caesar's and to God that which is God's." Jesus knew we had to live in society and to attend to our duties, and in that regard the ego can be a facilitator. He tried to teach discernment to his disciples so that they knew when to rely on their ego and when to call upon the transcendent. We need to heed this lesson as well.

I can't count the times I have heard someone in therapy tell me, "I just want to get rid of my ego." Even more frequently, clients want to "get rid" of their shyness, or low self-esteem, or anger, or whatever aspect of their personality that's troubling them. They are usually disappointed when I tell them they can't get rid of themselves. The prevailing opinion of those in therapy, especially those practicing spiritual disciplines, is that the ego is the crux of every problem.

In truth we would never survive in the world without our ego. It is the part of our personality that makes choices and directs mental traffic. It receives input from the senses about the environment and helps us meet our needs by organizing this data and processing it. The ego also draws on our memory of past actions and results so that we can make appropriate choices. It is the repository of our attitudes and beliefs about life and even about itself. The ego alerts us to danger, protects us from injury, and its habitual ways of dealing with everyday affairs is vital to our survival. It also comprises our instinctive responses to life situations. For example, if a car approaches us at a street crossing, the ego at an unconscious level ascertains the threat and takes action if necessary. Cerebral processes would be far too slow to analyze the threat and avoid the danger.

The child's ego develops as it grows. A parent's

watchfulness is a surrogate at this stage, not allowing a child near staircases and hot stoves, holding hands crossing streets and strapping him or her into the car seat. This is a gradual learning and conditioning process that at some point the child's ego develops enough to take over. All the childhood traumas get built in as well as those fleeting transcendent moments. Hopefully a healthy ego develops, balanced between the needs of the outside and inside worlds. Those on a spiritual path or one of self-development need a particularly strong but flexible ego structure. If we are mentally or emotionally unsteady, the first order of business is to strengthen our ego and its' functioning through spiritual practice and/or therapy. Unstable people don't have strong boundaries. They have a tendency to merge with the collective unconscious and lose their identity, whatever their spiritual orientation. To enter transcendent states and return to operate in our daily lives takes a great balancing act. The following story illustrates the dangers of not relying on the ego at certain times.

Why Didn't You Hiss?

A holy man visited a small village in India. After he paid his respects in their modest Shiva Temple, he was given water with which to bathe and food to eat. Following his rest, a group of villagers sat around him eager to hear his wise stories and receive his blessing. The next day as he was ready to depart, the villagers warned him not to leave town by way of a certain road. Ignoring their requests, he followed this path. The villagers called out to him to leave by way of the forest rather than get caught by a vicious snake. The village children were taught never to play near the road, and no one ever dared to set foot on it. Undaunted the holy man proceeded on his way. Eventually he met the vicious snake that recognized his spiritual stature and asked for his blessing and help. The holy man gave the snake darshan or spiritual advice and continued on his way. Embolden by the holy man's disregard, a few adventurous children snuck down the road weeks later to see the snake. The bravest of them even walked up to him. Unlike its previous behavior, the snake didn't threaten the children. Eventually a few boys tagged the snake. Again he ignored their play. Finally, the bravest of them grabbed the snake and twirled him around without getting bit.

Years passed and the holy man returned to the small village. As he walked down the road, the snake cried out to him. The saint didn't recognize the snake. It was battered beyond recognition. He asked what had happened. The snake told his sad story of how the vicious village children grew bolder and bolder, eventually shaking, throwing, and stomping on him. The snake tried not to take offense but this only emboldened them. After severely abusing the snake this way, they tossed him by the side of the road leaving him for dead. After that the snake hid from the children as the road became open once again. The holy man was puzzled by the snake's behavior. He asked why it allowed this abuse by the children. The snake replied that it wanted to be spiritual and not bite children or villagers after receiving darshan from the saint on his last visit. The holy man shook his head, "Well, you didn't have to bite, you could have just hissed."[19]

The snake made the opposite mistake of Prince Five-Weapons. It relied on its spirituality to deal with a hostile

---

[19] Anandi Ma

environment. It needed the resources of its ego to contend with the vicious children. This is similar to the devotee that got stomped by the elephant while all the onlookers tried to deter him. Both of them needed the ego's defensive protection to stave off physical harm. When I tell clients such stories, many respond that they would never be so stupid. My experience tells me otherwise.

Spiritual Bypassing

Churches are filled with multitudes praying to God for the alleviation of troubles they have brought on themselves by not dealing with life challenges intelligently. We need to use our innate intelligence to perceive reality and interpret the feedback. It can help us to know our weaknesses and strengths, and alert us when beliefs or emotions are distorting the information we're trying to interpret. We need to be discerning so that we appropriately use the resources of our ego or call upon the potentiality of the Self to deal with a problem.

Our recently inspired snake made a major error in judgment. It should have used the defenses of its ego to protect itself and allow it access to a transcendent state. It could've hissed to protect its higher self. God won't do that job for us. That's why we develop an ego to survive in the world and take care of ourselves so as to create a sacred space for our leaps of consciousness. But that can also create a problem. As we evolve our consciousness, we encounter the danger that these experiences can be so alluring that we can forget how to function effectively in everyday life. States of divine love and harmony can be ecstatic and leave us seeing everything as "rosy." *The Bhagavad Gita* admonishes us, "Not by mere renunciation does [man] attain supreme freedom. . . .

Perform therefore thy task in life. . . . The world is in the bonds of action, let thy actions be pure."[20]

A dilemma I frequently encounter with those who have begun their spiritual awakening is that they often unknowingly rely on a spiritual perspective to solve problems best reserved for the ego and its defenses.

The Spiritual Doormat

Naomi was typical of many I have counseled who unconsciously hid behind their spirituality when they need to engage life with other personality resources. She was a woman in her mid-thirties who was very spiritual and truly lived her spirituality. Naomi attended a small metaphysical church and helped the minister meet the needs of a growing congregation. She worked part time hosting parties for children and earned money as an intuitive, a very talented psychic who helped her clients with guidance and support. She also gave meditation workshops to small groups of people and generously shared her spiritual gifts.

But Naomi had difficulty dealing with the more mundane aspects of life. Although she was an excellent intuitive, she was lax about charging for her services and reluctant to ask for a fee if a client didn't pay. She had a basket on a table in her waiting room with a sign that read, "kindly leave a donation." Many just ignored the request. Naomi typically received many calls at night for help, often spending an hour or two giving free advice, sometimes talking late into the evening. She also was in a relationship with a man who treated her poorly and was inconsiderate of her time and

---

[20] *The Bhagavad Gita.* 3.8,9

space. He would drop by without notice, spend the night, and then not call for weeks. On occasion he would cancel a date at the last minute without a good explanation.

When I first met Naomi, she told me that she loved her psychic counseling but was drained by the demands it made on her. She wanted to share her gifts, and while she claimed it wasn't spiritual to demand money, Naomi was at a crisis point financially and didn't know how to proceed. Another problem, which was actually similar in some regards, was her boyfriend's attitude and his inconsiderate treatment of her. In both cases, she was being taken for granted, whether she could see that or not.

We discussed her situation, and I told her that she had very weak boundaries. She needed to use the word "no"' more often and set limits with her clients. I suggested that she change the sign in her waiting room to a given amount per hour, to be paid at the end of each session. I explained how she was co-creating the way her boyfriend treated her by not sharing her feelings about his behavior and setting some ground rules. Initially Naomi was upset with my suggestions, saying that they weren't "spiritual." I then introduced her to a concept called "spiritual bypassing." It means that the individual isn't properly integrating spirituality into their daily life, and that they are unfairly asking Spirit to perform some of the duties of their ego, like protecting themselves against encroachment.

After resisting my initial suggestions, Naomi continued in the same vein, becoming more drained by both her work and the abusive relationship with her boyfriend. However, she kept up with her therapy and eventually began to realize that she suffered from low self-esteem and didn't feel equal to others in relationships. She gave too much of herself to compensate for her feelings of inferiority and became further drained by this effort. The one source of positive feedback was her psychic counseling work, but it was as if she were afraid to jeopardize that by charging regularly for her services. It also didn't bolster her enough to confront her boyfriend about his abusive treatment. After a while it became obvious that the real resistance was her faulty understanding of the dual nature of spirituality.

Over several sessions, I explained how she was ungrounded and escaped into the Sacred within herself and devalued her experience in the world as not a sacred province. However, a great many Western and Eastern religions teach that God is not only transcendent but is immanent in creation as well. Naomi and many like her tend to escape into the God within and lose contact with God immanent in the world, or that everything including ourselves is sacred and an expression of God. To allow others to treat us in a demeaning manner denies the God in us and in them. The ego in its highest functioning could be considered a guardian of that principle. By protecting us from encroachment, it allows us to nurture ourselves and to further develop the Godhead within us. By developing a strong ego with healthy boundaries, we can better integrate the Sacred into every waking moment.

This new understanding energized Naomi and she began to change her attitude about herself. She came to realize that, especially in regard to her psychic counseling, not honoring her efforts with monetary compensation was not only an insult to her but to the God within her in whose name she provided this service. In regards to her boyfriend, she was worthy of better treatment. While she had her faults and weaknesses, she needed others to treat her and for her to treat others with more respect. This led to confrontations in both arenas, but Naomi stood her ground this time. While she lost some business along with her erstwhile boyfriend, she began to feel more lively and happier, and she enjoyed her life more.

Naomi's story is similar to many other spiritually inclined people I meet. We can't count on God to fix what the ego is meant to handle. We need to be careful of spiritual bypassing. In fact, this is a way of developing a healthy ego. Entrusting it to be the guardian of the Sacred puts it into a proper relationship with other aspects of the Self, not making it the sole focus. "There is a wisdom which knows when to go and when to return, what is to be done and what is not to be done, what is fear and what is courage, what is bondage and what is liberation—that is pure wisdom."[21]

Buddha echoed Krishna's words when he said, "Do not fail to do what ought to be done, and do not do what ought not to be done. Otherwise, your burden of suffering will grow heavier. Those who meditate and keep their senses under control never fail to do what ought to be done, and never do what ought not to be done. Their suffering will come to an end."[22]

Reason and Spirituality

Indian philosophy, particularly Vedanta, explains that man proceeds from lower to higher truths. The necessity of the creation from man's viewpoint is to lead him higher and higher until he brings out all the powers latent in him.

---

[21] Ibid. 18.30
[22] Ibid. 4.35,42

Mankind understands that life is its classroom and every experience is important to its development. This philosophy of life includes the laws of evolution and causation in which we see God's immanence. In fact, they are one and the same. God is Law and God is Consciousness. There is no conflict. I am reminded of the renowned Jesuit priest, Teilhard de Chardin, a paleontologist and spiritual giant who wrote of man's evolution. He regarded man as on an ascent of consciousness, which ultimately led to what he called the *Omega Point* (God). He was one of the first Christian spiritual teachers to embrace science and religion and synthesize the two. However, Indian philosophy has always honored both disciplines. It requires man to use his rational mind to understand himself in relationship to the world. The importance of reason in *The Bhagavad Gita* is great. Krishna tells Arjuna, "When wisdom is thine, Arjuna, never more shalt thou be in confusion . . . kill therefore with the sword of wisdom the doubt born of ignorance. Be one in self-harmony in Yoga, and arise, great warrior arise."[23]

When we properly use our intellect, we can avoid the problems highlighted in this chapter. Prince Five-Weapons made the mistake of not calling on his Self, relying on his ego resources until he was in the throes of death. On the other hand, Naomi did not use the designs of her ego to support and honor her spirituality until her spiritual bypass brought her to counseling. The Taoist concept of the Yin and the Yang shows the importance of two dynamic principles working together to create and sustain the world. The same applies to Spirit and Ego working together within us to

---

[23] Ibid

sustain and fulfill our lives.

Chapter Five
The Ego's Balancing Act

I was in the eighth grade when a girl named Rita busted me. "Don. You think you're such hot stuff when you're with your friends; you act like a real ass. Why can't you just be yourself all the time?" I knew she was right because her remark floored me. I turned red in the face, mumbled a defense, and shuffled away. I didn't think of myself as stuck-up. Even as a thirteen-year-old, I knew better. But that's not how others saw me.

Most of us don't like to think that we have a big ego. We consider ourselves good people, accepting of others at all times. But, when the ego or little self is in charge, pride can sneak up on us, usually when we are least aware of it. Pride has been called one of the seven deadly sins for a good reason. It isolates us from ourselves, others, and even from divine love. It often flares up when we don't deal with our feelings, especially of rejection or hurt, and we compensate by thinking we're better than others, or that the rules don't apply to us. Every sacred text I've studied warns about the dangers of pride. In every tradition, spiritual teachers have expounded on this subject. One story I particularly like is found in the Gospel of St. Luke.

Mary and Martha

Jesus visited the house of Mary and Martha with a number of His disciples. Upon His arrival, Mary was filled with such ecstatic happiness that she "fell upon the Lord's countenance."

The other sister, Martha, single-handedly cooked and set out the food to feed Jesus and his disciples. When she met the Lord, she complained to the Master, "Please judge for yourself how wrong my sister Mary is. She is sitting in the room doing nothing and I am doing all these things by myself." Jesus said, *"Mary is indeed blessed; she has developed the only thing needful in human life: love of God."*[1]

This story teaches that we cut ourselves off from God, not the reverse. Martha was entertaining the Lord in her house, but her jealousy and pride brought a just rebuke from Jesus. She had an opportunity to humbly serve the Lord but instead she strove to honor herself and not her love of God. She experienced humiliation when she could have created a loving bond with the Divine. God's love is omnipresent; our ability to receive it is not.

We act like Martha when we feel or act superior to those around us. Our ego seeks to enhance itself by speaking ill or playing a game of one-upmanship with others. The Microcosm (man's soul) separates itself from the Macrocosm

---

[1] *Holy Bible*. Luke. 10.38

(God) when the ego inflates itself. Krishna adroitly said, "The yogi who sees himself in the heart of all beings and sees all being in his heart . . . *then I never leave him and he never leaves me.*[2]

When my ego was there, there was no God,
Now there's God and my ego is non existent
A single town Kabir asserts,
Two kings does not accommodate.[3]

The Dork That Dissed Others

Denny was a student at U.C. Santa Cruz and was flunking out of school. He came to see me because he was depressed about it. Denny was studying engineering at his parents' suggestion. He had been a good student in high school but was having trouble with the rigors of university studies, or this subject. I asked him why. He said, "Don, the teachers don't know how to teach. They aren't organized and ramble on. They shouldn't be teaching at all. The university would fire them if they heard one of them lecture."

"Why don't the other students have the same trouble if the teachers are that bad?"

"You don't know what the other kids are like," he said. "They study day and night and don't have a life. I'd rather flunk than be a dork like them."

I replied, "You seem to diss the kids and teachers; maybe you need to ask yourself, how can all of them be dorks? From

---

[2]   *The Bhagavad Gita*, Juan Mascaro. 6.30. 1985.Penguine Classics. N.Y., N.Y

[3]   Kari, Mohan Singh. 2006. *Kabir*. 5. 4-5 New Delhi, India: Motil Banaarsidass Pub. Pvt. Ltd.

what you told me, you were something of a dork in high school."

Denny dismissed my remarks; he probably thought I was a dork. But he continued to vent his feelings about the university and the teachers. We met several times and finally he admitted that he wasn't a good engineering student. Eventually he changed his major and his grades improved greatly. The next semester I asked him what he thought about the university. He said he liked it and thought everybody was pretty cool.

As long as Denny was criticizing others, he didn't look at himself. Because he felt inadequate about his low grades, he denigrated those around him to feel better. However, his depression, as is often the case, forced him to address the underlying issues.

The Divine Mother Slays Two Demons

From the dawn of time, we humans have struggled with our ego, and today that conflict continues in a modern guise. The epic battle between the ego and the Self has been depicted in spiritual stories through the ages as the clash between the armies of good and evil, or that of powerful Gods facing off against one another. We have already shown how, in *The Bhagavad Gita,* Krishna used the battlefield as the staging ground for teaching Arjuna. A favorite story of mine is a battle between the mightiest of Gods in the heavens, to remind us that to vanquish the ego we have to take up the sword against it. The wording may be a bit highfalutin and the language arcane, but the message is clear. We need to brandish our sharpest weapons and prepare for a long and arduous fight to defeat the demons within us.

Approximately 900 B.C. the *Durga Saptasti* or *Chandi Pathah* was first told, although it didn't appear in written form until centuries later. You may recall that in the story of Indra discovering his True Self, he was accompanied on his journey by an Asura who misunderstood the lesson and vowed to serve the ego. In this story the Asuras are very powerful Gods, and a battle takes place between them and the Divine Mother. Chapter Ten recounts how the Divine Mother *Camunda*, also known as *She Who Tears Apart Thought*, slays *Khaitabha*, known as Self-Conceit and *Madhu*, Self-Depreciation.

"The rishi said: The Goddess and Self-Conceit began a dreadful battle . . . with showers of arrows, sharp weapons and incredible missiles, the combat which engaged them was frightful to all the worlds. The Mother of the Universe discharged hundreds of divine missiles, which were cut by Khaitabha's defensive weapons . . . the Goddess in anger cut his bow with Her arrows. With his bow broken, Khaitabha took up his energy in the form of lightening, but that was cut by the Goddess with Her discus while it was still in his hand. Khaitabha took his brilliant sword and shield bearing a hundred moons, and rushed toward the Goddess. As he was approaching, *She Who Tears Apart Thought* waged battle with him with all her weapons. Camunda began to fight in the atmosphere as never before, causing astonishment to adepts and men of wisdom. Madhu, known as Self-Depreciation, took up battle alongside his brother. After a long close encounter, the Mother raised him above, spun him around, and threw him to the ground. Thus thrown to the earth, he hastily got up, and raising his fist, that wicked one rushed forward to kill *She Who Tears Apart Thought* . . . Seeing the approach of Madhu, the Goddess pierced him in the chest with Her pike and threw him again to the earth. Pierced by the sharp point of the Goddess's pike, he fell dead upon the ground, shaking the entire earth with its oceans, its islands and its mountains . . ."[4] "When the Asuras of Thought were slain by the Goddess, the Gods with the Rule of the Pure, led by the Light of Meditation, illuminated the heavens with their cheerful faces . . . and praised the Ever Pure One."[5]

Note that even the demigods were troubled with thoughts of self-conceit. That is how powerful an adversary's thoughts were considered. The *Chandi Pathah* continues with a recitation of appreciation and adoration to the Goddess. Chapter Ten ends when the Goddess tells the heavens that at the end of an epoch, the demon will return and haunt the lower world (earth). Camunda promises that She will return to help mankind as the Goddess Kali. Today many sincere devotees of the Goddess recite the *Chandi Pathah* daily or perform puja (ceremony) to Kali in what is known as *Kali Puja*. To those who perform this rite, or to anyone who calls on Her in earnest, She aids them in their struggle against Self-Depreciation and Self-Conceit.

The Ethical Excuse Clause

Pride slips past our self-awareness in many ways. A modern Khaitabha uses ethical and moral one-upmanship effectively. A number of years ago, I managed a brokerage office and had a dozen sales reps working for me. One of my duties was to review security trades by the reps to ensure that

---

[4]   Swami Satyananda Saraswati.*Chandi Patah* Ch. 10 10-27. 1985 Devi Mandir. Napa, CA

[5]   Ibid. Ch. 10.27

they were in the best interests of our clients. If I thought a transaction was too speculative or questionable, I would review the investors' objectives and risk tolerance with the broker who made the trade. With rare exception the salespeople in my office followed good ethical principles. The office's sales production generated a normal bell curve.

The top sales producer in my office was a diligent young man with about five years of experience. He often worked late into the night talking to clients and prospects, earning his success the hard way. A few of the salespeople in the office were jealous of his production and the large income he earned. They nicknamed him "Churn" and accused him of making trades solely for commissions. I talked to these salespeople a number of times, telling them to stop the name-calling. The verbal swipes stopped, but their jealousy ran deep and showed up in other ways.

They justified their lower sales by saying they had their client's best interest at heart and would never stoop to "churning" someone in and out of trades to raise their own sales. They were claiming to be ethically superior to justify their own poor performance. When I confronted them on their work habits, they claimed they were more knowledgeable about investments and didn't need to work long hours to service their accounts. I didn't need to state the obvious, that they were attracting less new business. They were unwilling to question their own work habits or so-called expertise, but would rather denigrate a colleague with more drive and ingenuity to cover any fears or doubts about their own competence. They would've been better served if they had read a little more Kabir and less of the *Wall Street Journal*.

I set out in search of the bad

No one who was bad did I see,
As much as I do introspect
There is no one so bad as me.[6]

The Sannyasi's Lady of Ill Repute

The ego will use any means to inflate itself. Religion, spirituality, morality, and ethics are no exception. Sacred texts and stories through the ages warn us about falling into the trap of spiritual pride. It is considered the worst type of self-conceit.

There was once a lady of ill repute who lived across the street from a temple. A sannyasi (holy man) living in the temple came to her one day and said, "You are living a contemptible life. I want to show you the heaps of your sins. For every visitor that comes to see you, I am going to put down a stone." And he did. He sat on the temple steps and watched who came and went from that lady's house. With every visitor, the sannyasi placed a stone in a pile on the steps.

The woman eventually said, "Oh my God, will you ever forgive me? What else can I do with my life? I don't know any other means to make a living. But, look at all of those stones there."

Meanwhile, the sannyasi sat in the temple and complained, "That damnable woman! Look at the heaps of sins that she is piling up."

Through the years this continued until there was virtually a mountain of stones and "sins" piled up in front of the

---

[6] Kari, Mohan Singh. 2006. *Kabir*. 32.#5 New Delhi, India: Motil Banaarsidass Pub. Pvt. Ltd.

temple. The poor woman was totally distraught and constantly in prayer implored, "Dear Lord, please forgive me, but show me another way and I will be glad to follow it."

One day a carriage came racing down the street, ran over the woman, and she died. All the citizens of the town proclaimed, "What a relief! All of those sins are gone from our community."

It just so happened that the sannyasi died on the same day. The townspeople threw the body of the lady of ill repute out beyond the gates, where it was torn apart and devoured by wild dogs. With a brass band, they carried the sannyasi on a silk stretcher, covered with flowers, and marched him around the town. They ended up at the burning ghats on the side of the river where they cremated his body with sandalwood. His soul went up to heaven. When God saw him, he asked, "What are you doing here? You don't belong here."

The sannyasi cried out, "What do you mean, I don't belong here? I lived in the temple all my entire life."

God said, "Yes. Your body may have lived in the temple, but your mind was constantly across the street with the prostitute. You go to hell. She is coming to heaven. Even though her body was engaged in those irreligious acts, her mind was constantly begging for forgiveness. Therefore, she deserves a place in heaven. You go."[7]

Spiritual pride applies not only to individuals, but also to religions claiming to be the only route to personal salvation. It can even provoke religious wars to kill and maim "heathens" who don't adhere to their beliefs. I was raised

---

[7] The Gospel of Sri Ramakrishna. Nikhilananda. P.201. Ramakrishna-Vivekananda Center. 2000.

Catholic and attended parochial schools in the 1950s. As a child I was taught that we belonged to the one true religion and that other religious beliefs were false. We were told that only Catholics were allowed into heaven. We had been chosen by God. That teaching was confusing to me. I was troubled by the fact that many of the good people around me couldn't go to heaven because they weren't Catholic. As a child I was never able to reconcile the fact that God played favorites. After expanding my own religious education and after reading the previous story, I've always wondered what awaits those who claim God for themselves. Hindus would say they're coming back next time as "heathens" to reconcile previously held beliefs. That's a heartening idea.

Abba Prior's Bag of Sins

When we point an accusing finger at others, we ignore our own personal issues. We keep them in what Jung referred to as the shadow part of our personality, a kind of rejection dustbin, outside of our conscious awareness. There they exert psychological pressure, which we often try to relieve by projecting them onto others. For instance, if I'm uncomfortable with some aspect of my personality, I may unknowingly look for that same imperfection in someone else. I sometimes think of it as a teeter-totter. The less I have accepted my own imperfections, the more I am going to find them outside myself. Abba Prior knew this only too well.

As Abba Prior entered a room in the abbey, he heard a lot of indignation about a brother they were accusing of committing a sin. The brothers were severely rebuking the sinner, who had admitted his offense but found no forgiveness in the others. As the Abba entered, the monks told him what had transpired, expecting him to join them in their castigation of the sinner. The Abba remained silent and after a few minutes left the room without saying a word to the others. He went outside, took a large sack and filled it with sand. He then took a much smaller bag and filled it. As he reentered the room, Abba Prior dragged the heavy sack behind him while holding the small bag in front of him.

When the brothers asked him the meaning of this demonstration, Abba Prior said, "In this sack, which contains much sand, are my sins which are many; I have put them behind me so as not to be troubled by them and to weep about them. Here in this little bag are the small sins of the same nature committed by my brother, which are in front of me. Why should I spend my time judging them when they are but a reflection of my own sins that are even heavier? This is not right. If I am in the mood to judge, I ought carry my own sins in front of me and concern myself with them."[8]

It takes a high degree of self-awareness and personal discipline to attain the wisdom of a Brother Prior. The road to that level of awareness is an arduous path as the couple in the following story discovered.

I'm Better Than You

My client Bonnie once told me that she wanted to work to improve her marriage. I told her I'd be glad to offer whatever help I could. She introduced me to her husband Jake, who was a tall man with a scholarly demeanor. He was a little defensive when I first met him. Jake and Bonnie had known each other since their college days, when he was an

---

[8] *Desert Fathers*. Poeman 64. Cistercian Publications. 1975

engineering student and she was studying to be a teacher. They shared the same goals and were idealistic in a grounded and practical way. Over the years, they adopted two children from third-world countries and were passionate about their children's education and character formation. But in spite of their shared goals, both Bonnie and Jake felt that they were now drifting apart and didn't feel the closeness they expected from their marriage as they matured.

As we started couples therapy, I found that Jake was highly critical of Bonnie. He complained about everything she did from being forgetful, not adhering to time schedules, to being a poor homemaker. Jake expected her to perform her daily activities with the same engineering preciseness that he brought to his job. If the sink wasn't cleaned a certain way, he jumped on her. If Bonnie was late for an appointment, he browbeat her. If their checkbook didn't balance, he got upset. Bonnie couldn't do anything right from Jake's point of view. While Jake complained about Bonnie in our sessions, she kept making excuses for her incompetence that only made him angrier.

It was soon clear to me, or to anyone except Jake, that his criticism of Bonnie was the source of their difficulties. He solidified his position through one-upmanship, and Bonnie unwittingly accepted her position under him on the ladder.

I finally asked Jake why he had to be the expert and make all the decisions in the marriage. He told me that someone had to take charge of the situation, or it would be a mess otherwise. Jake said that by training he was mentally sharper and could find solutions more quickly, so it was natural that he should call the shots.

I then asked Bonnie why she constantly acquiesced to her husband, and she said that he was smarter than her. When I asked if she had different talents from Jake, she replied that she did but they were not as useful as Jake's. Bonnie was a grade school teacher, a storyteller at the library; she had some theater experience and was in charge of school plays.

I asked Jake what he thought about his wife's creativity. He said he believed in a hierarchy of gifts and considered certain talents, such as his wife's creativity, less critical to the family's welfare than his ability to earn a good living. Basically Jake considered himself superior to his wife because of his education, intelligence, and well-paying job.

Bonnie, for her part, needed to rethink the value of what she contributed to her family and to the community at large. Her nurturing gifts of gentleness, compassion, and love were the thriving heart of their home and the emotional center of her children's and her husband's lives, whether he would acknowledge it or not. It was unfair to devalue such an important if intangible contribution to her family's welfare, just because Jake brought home the bacon.

Our society in its outward manifestation is decidedly male-oriented, rewarding left-brain and practical gifts such as math and science skills and their application over the more cultivating value of the humanities. There is a tendency to devalue the latter as inferior studies or contributions to society, or at least in areas other than literature, art, and film. Jake looked down on his wife because he had traits and abilities that our society prizes in general and she didn't, or at least not overtly.

Their marriage was bearing a great strain because of his haughtiness. I pointed out to both Bonnie and Jake that while their talents might be very different from each other's, that there was no higher or lower talent. Within any society, including a family, such talents and abilities were usually a compensatory and not a hierarchical exchange. While Jake's job might support their family, try performing it well on TV dinners, wearing dirty clothes, or being horny all the time. And while Jake clothed his children, Bonnie was the emotional center of their lives.

Jake had great difficulty with this train of thought. He had grown up in an environment that taught him differently, but he was intelligent and eventually couldn't deny the logic of this approach. Jake began to gradually accept that they each made their own important contributions to each other's and their family's welfare. He couldn't judge his contributions or himself as better than his wife. Eventually Jake made some needed concessions in the marriage, even if he had trouble internalizing the new beliefs. He was able to see the cost his outmoded ideas had on the marriage and made sincere efforts to change them.

Ego Inflation and Judgment

It is important that we don't discard the good with the bad. We need feedback from life to make intelligent decisions. Value judgments are an important part of this process. Before I send my child to a tutoring service, I may sift through a list of names and get feedback from friends about their experiences with different teachers. Some will do a better job than others, or will be better for different subjects. I want to be an intelligent consumer, especially where my child's welfare is concerned. There is nothing inherently wrong with such a winnowing process. I can only be faulted, or commit the sin of pride, if I denigrate a teacher as a human being because someone else is more proficient in their work. When we demean someone in this manner, we have added emotional judgment to the decision process. You can rarely judge a person's humanity by their job performance. Just look at some of the highly successful people in our society and tell me differently.

One of the most direct and poignant spiritual messages ever given, and one that cuts to the core of ego inflation, was spoken by Jesus: "Judge not that you not be judged. For with the judgment you pronounce you will be judged, and the measure you give will be the measure you get. Why do you see the speck that is in your brother's eye, but do not notice the log that is in your own? Or how can you say to your brother let me take the speck out of your eye, when there is a log in your own eye."[9]

Jesus understood that it is easier to criticize our brother than to acknowledge and change our own weaknesses. He knew that everyone had to work on their own personal, spiritual, and moral growth. Focusing our attention on the speck in our brother's eye distracts us from the log in our own. More than once in the New Testament, Jesus admonished his followers to examine their own frailties before condemning others. For instance, as the angry mob was about to stone the prostitute, Jesus said, "Let he who is without sin cast the first stone." Everyone stopped, cast their eyes down, dropped their stones, and walked away.

Emotional reaction is the key to spotting ego inflation. If I disagree with my friend's political stance, that in itself shouldn't be a problem for either of us. However, if I consider his opinion unintelligent merely because it differs from mine, then I have engaged in ego one-upmanship. Opinions are simply opinions. Recently I was guilty of much

---

[9] *Holy Bible*. Matthew 7-4

the same. I was telling an intelligent friend of mine, who often called those who disagreed with him dumb, to be less judgmental. We actually got into an argument about this, and I found myself judging him inferior for judging others, thus making the same mistake. I mentioned earlier that pride is one of the seven deadly sins for this very reason—it easily slips under our radar screen. I still can't believe I was judging him for judging others in the same manner.

The Divine in Me, the Divine in You

We easily confuse performance with beingness. The spark of the divine that is in me is the same as the spark of divine that is in my friend. There is no qualitative or quantitative difference. I may be highly spiritual and my friend may be caught in the entrapment of various addictions and not manifesting his Higher Self, but we are both fully human and fully divine, neither better than the other. In *The Bhagavad Gita*, Krishna admonished Arjuna to do his duty no matter how grand or humble the task. He was to follow his dharma and not to judge others following theirs. "I am equally present in all beings; there is none hateful or dear to me."[10]

Anandi Ma tells the wonderful story of a well-renowned guru and his disciples at a particular ashram with a very large following. As with any organization, there were a great many duties that needed attention. Some devotees had duties that were of personal service to the guru. Others kept his home clean or worked in his kitchen. These duties were prized because they put the devotees in close physical contact with the guru. Some of these devotees had been taking guidance

---

[10] *The Bhagavad Gita.* 8.23

from him for a long period of time and were quite advanced in their spiritual practices.

One day the guru told his disciples that he would be taking a long trip and would appoint someone to take his place while he was absent. While the devotees were saddened by the news, some were hopeful that the mantel of responsibility would be placed on their shoulders. Many of them were competent and intelligent and had personally served the guru for many years. When the guru announced that a disciple outside their inner circle would be placed in charge, a moan was heard throughout the ashram. The chosen individual was uneducated, considered slow-witted, and had no experience running a large ashram.

The guru left on his trip and many of his disciples immediately deserted the ashram. They were at a loss to understand their teacher's decision and refused to take directions from his appointee. Many members of the inner circle with important jobs left. Soon there was no one doing housecleaning, cooking, or taking care of important ashram work. The poor disciple in charge kept praying, "Dear Lord, I am very dumb and don't know how to cook, I don't know how to organize a household, please help me."

The Gods heard his plea and because his love of God was so pure and deep, the Goddess of Households along with other Gods came to the ashram and performed these duties. Several months later, the guru returned and fell at the feet of the disciple he had left in charge. He said, "I only had students perform the daily household chores, but you are so pure and close to the Lord that She herself came to help. You are the highest teacher; let me be your disciple."

Our Self is the Microcosm of the Macrocosm. All of us are identical. Some have probed deeper into the Self and have experienced more of It than others. *This only means that they enjoy the qualities of the Godhead: peace, joy, love, quietude, happiness, and spiritual connection more fully. They are not superior to others who are caught in life's snares. No matter how completely some have realized God. The same Soul` resides in each one of us. There is no higher or lower.*

The Little Girl Who Liked the Devil

Depending on one's life-plan (our dharma), some are troubled by ego deflation rather than inflation. Their struggle is to realize that they are just as good as their neighbor. They suffer from a deep sense of inadequacy. As a therapist I have counseled many individuals who suffered from low self-esteem. The seeds of self-depreciation are usually sown very early in life. I had no idea just how early until a young child, I'll call Laura, visited my office with her mother. Laura had been kicked out of preschool. The child was very hyper and talkative in my office. In no time she was happily bouncing around on my couch, and her mother had to restrain her. I was finally able to ask Laura some questions about what made her happy and what made her sad. She didn't like school because she always got into trouble for some reason or other. When her mother talked with her teachers, she usually yelled at Laura for being naughty which she didn't like either. I then asked Laura what she did like. She answered, "I like the Devil."

"Laura, why do you like the Devil?" I asked.

"Because he's bad and I'm bad, too." I then asked Laura why she was bad. She said, "Because I don't do what my mother tells me."

I had not expected our conversation to take that turn and I was caught off guard. The conversation stayed with me for days as I realized just how early in life our self-image can be negatively influenced. Eventually, I was able to get to the root of Laura's rebellious behavior, due to poor class performance, and address her issues early enough so as not to form a permanent imprint on her personality. The same can't be said for many others whose early childhood experiences leave them with low self-esteem for life. In such cases a religious education comes too late to open them to their inner divinity, one that they never felt worthy enough to contact. In such cases, they live a lie, treat themselves poorly, and can never reach for all the richness that life may offer them.

"In the Circle All Things Are Related"

The American Indian tradition holds beliefs very similar to Hinduism and Buddhism. It considers all life sacred and permeated by God's Consciousness. Cherokee teachings tell us we are all here for a reason. Each of us has a special purpose and reason for our existence. We don't know how the great web of life weaves together, nor do we fully understand our participation in it, but like chemical catalysts sometimes a small part of the whole can have a crucial impact on its survival. Life calls for weavers of diverse talents and gifts. Discord can happen when we look at our brother or sister and don't see their gifts, or when we judge them as less important than our own, or when we consider ours the lesser of the two. Consider the following:

"In the Native American way of understanding, the first illusion we are faced with is the illusion of pride, of superior and inferior. In the circle all things are related, neither up nor down. Nothing is alone, everything is together . . . We have a special purpose and a special reason for being here. In a journey to the *Temple of Understanding* we can clarify our understanding and come to a true knowing . . . superior and inferior is an illusion. The Temple of Understanding is within us and all around."[11]

Earlier we delved into the marriage difficulties of Jack and Bonnie. Jack underestimated his wife in part because she didn't demand respect. She believed her husband's opinions were better than her own, and that he was more important in their relationship because he earned more money. Bonnie's problem was a self-depreciation no doubt created years earlier by internalizing judgments made about her by others. She made the mistake of evaluating herself by quantitative measures. Young Laura didn't think she was as good as others because she didn't perform as well in class. The judgments of both Laura and Bonnie reflect the same theme. Both of them compared themselves to a standard or norm that they couldn't achieve and thus devalued themselves as individuals. They hadn't been taught or grasped the concept that each of us is unique and different and no one is higher or lower. According to Cherokee wisdom, "The first illusion we face is pride, of superior and inferior . . . in the circle all things are related, neither up nor down."[12] Each of us is an individual unit of God Consciousness. There is only one Self, the Creator, and we are the Microcosm of that Macrocosm.

Sita's Self-Improvement Project

A few years ago I counseled a young woman named Sita who was referred to me because of her depression. Sita was

---

[11] Dhyani Ywahoo. *Voices of Our Ancestors, Cherokee Teachings from the Wisdom of Fire*, Shambala. P.107. 1986

[12] Ibid. 107

very friendly and eager to understand herself. I asked if she enjoyed her life, and she told me she didn't get much pleasure out of most of her former activities. Sita was redecorating her house hoping this new venture would make her feel better. I asked her about her house project and was impressed by her industriousness. She had taken the doors off the kitchen cabinets and was sanding, staining, and putting a coat of polyurethane on them. She had also bought new hinges and knobs. Sita had purchased a sink and faucets, and planned to install them herself. And these were just a few of the home repairs she told me about.

I said, "Sita, you have a unique talent. It's awesome that you're doing all this redecoration without professional help."

"It's no big deal," she said, "I used to help my dad when I was young."

"Maybe so, but doing something this extensive alone is totally different; most handyman types I know wouldn't try such a project. I'm quite impressed."

The next time we met, Sita told me how she was going to replace the wallboards in the kitchen because they had too many nicks on them. She planned to buy the boards, prepare the surfaces, replace them, and then paint the entire room.

I said, "Sita that's a real project, are you going to get help with it?"

"I hadn't planned to; it's not so hard when you know how to do it."

Finally I told her, "Damn it Sita, you're doing a full remodeling of your kitchen by yourself, and every time I compliment you, you brush it away as if it's no big deal. I couldn't do anything that extensive, and I can't think of any of my friends who could do it either. I've probably complimented you a half-dozen times, but each time you dismiss it. Why are you unable to accept compliments?"

"Don, like I told you," she said, "I learned to do it early on and it's no big deal."

I said to Sita, "The things you do very well, actually exceptionally well, you don't acknowledge. You dismiss them by saying you learned them from your father. I used to work with my father too, but I couldn't remodel my kitchen today. It is important to acknowledge your talent as a home-improvement decorator. On the other hand, you're always comparing yourself to other women who are more socially adept or better educated, putting yourself down. You compare yourself to others in their area of expertise and feel inadequate, yet you dismiss your own talents as not equal to theirs, just because you have special training. So did they; their mothers help them develop such skills, and some of them probably went to finishing schools as young girls. The fact is that we all have different abilities, and comparing them is unfair, like comparing apples and oranges. Each has its own place and balances out the whole."

Sita automatically rejected positive experiences, much the same as Bonnie did. It took time to weaken the beliefs of her inadequacy that kept her bound. We had many discussions, and gradually Sita identified the feelings of her negative self-image that wouldn't allow an acceptance of the "good stuff," as she clung to the "bad stuff." It took awhile for a shift in her attitude to occur. Bonnie, Laura, and Sita compared themselves negatively to others with different talents, abilities, or traits that they lacked, and felt inadequate because of these unfavorable comparisons. They made the mistake of evaluating themselves on the basis of their performance against others or an arbitrary standard. Such mistaken evaluations are the curse of low self-esteem. Both Bonnie and

Sita had to work hard to change their self-concept and elevate their self-esteem. In spite of all their hard work, the old thought patterns were easily triggered. This frequently required them to raise the sword of self-knowledge to vanquish these old concepts, a task some of us are better at than others.

An "I Gotcha" Moment

In the *Chandi Pathah*, it took all the resources of the Goddess Camunda to slay the demons of Self-Conceit and Self-Depreciation. It took Bonnie a lot of diligent work to gain a solid footing with her husband, Jake. But she constantly had to be mindful of her own important contributions, and not let the mundane tasks of running a household allow self-depreciation to slip in the back door. While Sita gained a new appreciation of her unique talents and skills, a venture into the world of polite society could still intimidate her or trigger a memory of a past faux pas and erode her self-esteem. They had both learned that victory was never assured. They had to be ready to wage battle against their self-doubt whenever it reared its head. As mentioned earlier, the ego not only inflates (pride), but deflates (self-depreciation) us, different strategies that both keep us from engaging the Sacred within us.

Until we reach a sublime merger with the Divine, ego inflation and deflation will plagued us. There is no shame in this struggle; it's simply part of our path back to God. When I used to catch Khaitabha (Self-Conceit) making judgments in my head, I would often get angry for letting this slip by my awareness. I now realize that it is a normal function of my ego; I'll just step aside and watch it from a spiritual perspective, and its energy quickly dissipates. Sometimes I'll chuckle to myself and say, "I gotcha." Interestingly enough, I had a dream recently in which I was telling someone about Khaitabha and Madhu, and we both got caught off guard by a manifestation. In the dream I remarked, "See, how subtle this stuff is."

At the turn of the nineteenth century, a great scholar and spiritual giant by the name of Vivekenanda arose in India. He lectured widely in America to large audiences. William James, then president of Harvard, as well as scholars and intellectuals from England and America, traveled to India to listen to the swami's spiritual discourses. Speaking on the subject of knowledge, Vivekenanda said, "What thoughts and words frighten you? What thoughts and words make you weak? What makes you fear? Know that every thought and word that weakens you in this world is the only evil that exists . . . If the suns come down and the moons crumble into dust and systems after systems are hurled into annihilation, what is that to you? In this world of many, he who sees the One, in this ever changing world, he who sees Him who never changes, as the Soul of his own soul, as his own Self, he is free."[13]

---

[13] Swami Nikhilananda. Vivekananda *The Yogas and Other Works*. P.308. Ramadrishna-Vivekananda Ctr. NY. N.Y. 19

Chapter Six
Saving the Ego from Trickery and Deception

Most of us would like to prolong our healthy lives and enjoy the good experiences it brings. At heart we are pleasure-seeking people and this principle is fundamental to our growth as a species. Can you imagine our fate if making love was a disgusting and horrible experience? On the other hand, this programming can create a problem because the pursuit of pleasure can become uncontrollable. That which is pleasurable one day can cause us grief the next. Many desires can never be fully satiated and lead to obsessions. We need to be mindful of our tendency to overindulge life's desires. There is no clear line that separates healthy enjoyment from intemperance, and it is too easy to slip into excess. The following story tells of our all too human tendency to create such trouble.

The Ghost Named Greed

There was a poor man who was in need of money and was told that if he could get hold of a ghost, he would be able to command it to give him money. He searched far and wide and found a sage with yogic powers that could bring him a ghost. However, the yogi warned him that fulfilling his wish would be very dangerous, and he sent him away. The man returned the next day and pleaded with the yogi for a ghost, and finally, filled with disgust, the yogi gave in to the poor man's entreaty. The yogi said, "Be careful, ghosts are terrible beings and you have to keep them busy all the time. If you fail to do so, they will take your life."

Upon arriving home, the man was met by a ghost who told him, "I am a ghost, I have been conquered by your magic but you must keep me constantly employed. The moment you fail to do so, I will kill you."

The man said, "Build me a palace."

The ghost quickly returned from the countryside and said, "It is done, the palace is built."

"Bring me money," said the man. The ghost brought him money. The man became worried that he might not be able to keep this ghost busy. He told him, "Cut down this forest and build a large city."

A while later, the ghost appeared and said, "It is done, is there anything more?" The man became very frightened because the ghost worked so fast that he couldn't keep him occupied with work. The ghost warned him, "Give me something to do, or I will eat you."

The frightened man ran to the yogi in panic and said, "Save my life, I am about to die." The sage asked him what happened and the man told his sorrowful tale. Finally the yogi said, "I will help you if you have learned your lesson." The sage thought awhile and then said, "Do you see that dog with the curly tail? Draw your sword and cut off his tail and hand it to me." The man did as he was told. The sage instructed him, and he took the tail to the ghost and said, "[Straighten] it out." The ghost [straightened] out the tail and immediately it coiled again. The ghost diligently worked on the tail for days and days and finally said, "I am tired of this work, if you let me off I will not eat you." The man was much pleased and released the ghost from his promise."[1]

Our desires can easily torment us if we are not careful. The excessive pursuit of money has caused man to debase himself as much as any other obsession. In the following story, the ghost of greed got hold of Lyn and she nearly lost everything that she held dear.

Naomi and Her Hungry Ghost

Naomi was a well-dressed, gregarious, attractive forty-year-old mother of two boys. But the worry lines on her face betrayed the anxiety she held. When she arrived for her session, the first words out of her mouth were "I'm in serious trouble!"

Indeed as her story unfolded, she truly was in a fix. Naomi had been overspending for two years, and while she had so far hidden this liability from her husband, she was more than $30,000 in debt at this point.

What troubled her even more, she confessed, was that this was not the first time she had run up her credit cards. A number of years earlier, she had accumulated more than

---

[1]   *Vivekananda, The Yoga and Other Works.* Swami Nikhilananda. P.585 Ramakrishna Center N.Y. 1984.

$10,000 in bad debts that her husband had to pay off; he had warned her that if it happened again, he would leave her.

Naomi had a serious problem. I told her that I needed to sit down with her and her husband to help find a solution. She was scared about telling him and about bringing him in to see me, being afraid of what he might do. I told her that this was more than a personal dysfunction but also a marriage crisis, and that I couldn't solve one without addressing the other.

The next week a very frightened Naomi introduced me to her husband Chad, who I thought was quite a considerate and caring human being. He was nervous, and he told me that when Naomi insisted he come to her therapy session, he prepared himself for the worst.

I asked him what he thought the problem might be and he said, "Don, either she met another man, has cancer or a serious illness, or she's in debt again."

"Chad, it's the least of your three fears," I reassured him. "Naomi has gotten into debt again." He sat quietly for a while and then asked how much debt. I told him. Chad looked stunned and said he needed to step outside and think this through. He left the room. Naomi was in a panic; I reassured her, but the next ten minutes were the longest of her life.

Finally, the door opened and Chad came back in and took his seat. "Let's get down to business. I love my wife and family, and no one is going to die, so I suppose things could be worse." This startled Naomi as tears rolled down her cheeks. He decided the best course of action was to take out an equity line of credit on their house, consolidate a few other bills along with his wife's credit cards, and pay the line of credit as money came in.

This solution took a long and very trying therapy session

to work out. Naomi and Chad agreed that she would destroy all her credit cards, which she did in front of us, gave him the family checkbook, and agreed to meet regularly with me to review the situation. She left my office considerably relieved, but there was still work to do. Often the hungry ghost inside of us is a lack of self-worth, and the more we feed it "things," the more it grows and can consume our lives. Sometimes it takes a life-threatening or relationship-ending situation to face these demon ghosts and stop the feeding frenzy. In Naomi's case, it was not so much the threat of losing everything she held dear, but the incredible patience, kindness, and love of her husband that gave her the strength to "cut it off." This renewed their relationship and gave her a strong foundation to deal with the sense of lack inside of her, which we addressed in future sessions.

Naomi was fortunate that her husband prized her more than the security of money in the bank. The need to feed this hungry ghost with things she couldn't afford had nearly destroyed her family. While greed was the overt drive, and how she would have explained it before our sessions, it was her inner unresolved feelings of inadequacy from childhood that she masked with lust for possessions. Either way, obsessions divert us from the real task at hand and block the doorway to the Self. Runaway desires for riches, status, and possessions that mask inner emptiness have caused more ills for humankind than can be imagined. Such obsessions create a hell on earth for us and keep us separate from the divine. We dehumanize ourselves and those we exploit to satisfy our desires. Spiritual teachers continually warn us about our tendency to lose ourselves in these pursuits. Some sages have addressed it very directly. As Jesus once said, "If your right eye causes you to sin, pluck it out and throw it away; it is better that you lose one of your members than your whole body be thrown into hell. And if your right hand causes you to sin, cut it off and throw it away; it is better that you lose one of your members than your whole body go to hell."[2] The Buddha, upon his awakening, took a more gentle approach to helping people rise out of their misery. He was moved by the ignorance that caused us to suffer and set about teaching the dharma. The earliest recorded words Gotama the Buddha uttered following his enlightenment were, "All have I overcome, all do I know, from all am I detached, all have I renounced. *Wholly absorbed am I in the destruction of craving* . . . in the blind world I shall beat the drum of deathlessness."[3]

Once enlightened, the Buddha decided to teach the Dharma and left for Benares where he gave his first discourse the *Dhammacakkappavattana Sutta.* Dhamma-cadda means the founding of wisdom. The Four Noble Truths were first taught at this discourse. Truth one: everyone suffers; Truth two: *desire and craving are the source of suffering;* Truth three: there is a way to terminate suffering; and Truth four: the eightfold path . . . [4] which essentially consists of acquiring true wisdom as the way out of suffering.

Maharishi Patanjali, author of the *Yoga Sutras,* the original textbook of classical yoga, wrote in a style that was instructive in tone:

"Ignorance is the view that the ephemeral, the impure, the

---

[2] *Holy Bible.* Matt. 5.28-9

[3] *The Buddha and His Teachings.* Narada. P.68 Buddhist Pub. Society. Kandy. 1980

[4] *Yoga Sutras of Patanjali.* 11.5 Stiles. Weiser Books. Canada 2002

pain of suffering—that which is not the Self—is permanent, pure, pleasurable, and the true Self . . . there are five primal causes of suffering: ignorance of your True Self and the value of spirituality; egoism and its self centeredness; *attachment to pleasure*; aversion to pain; and clinging to life: out of fear of death."[5]

Spiritual teachers from all traditions repeat the one common theme that attachment to pleasure causes suffering. The key word is *attachment*. As we have seen, Krishna takes the middle ground on the issue of pleasure. We are advised to work hard and ground ourselves on planet earth. Pleasure is not to be avoided nor is it to be sought for its own sake. It is a part of life that we need to acknowledge and accept without becoming obsessed with it. Divine consciousness permeates everything and enjoying ourselves is no exception. All work, joy, suffering, pleasure, and the totality of human experiences are to be laid before the feet of God. He tells us to use our intellect to control the ego and its tendency to overindulge. The *Gita* and the *Vedas* tell us to keep pleasure-seeking within proper bounds. For those of us who raise families and go off to work every morning, this middle ground approach is most practical. But we still need to be mindful of the ego's tendencies to get carried away.

The Scorpion and the Holy Man

Once upon a time a holy man was taking his ritual bath in the river. He looked up and saw a scorpion struggling to stay afloat in the water. Being a compassionate man, he waded over in its direction to offer his help. He asked the scorpion

---

[5] Ibid. 11.3

what it was doing, and the scorpion told him that it wanted to reach the far shore. The holy man said he would carry him over, but was concerned that the scorpion might sting him.

"You have a bad reputation," he said. "I'm afraid if I help you, you may sting me."

The scorpion replied, "No sir, I would never sting you, I need your help to cross the river." As he reached over to pick up the scorpion, other men bathing in the river warned him about the danger.

The holy man told them, "This poor creature has reassured me that it won't sting me, so I will help it." No sooner had the holy man lifted the scorpion out of the water, than did it sting him. The holy man let go of the scorpion and both began to drown. The holy man resurfaced and lifted the scorpion and it stung him again. This happened several times. The scorpion did not let go of its need to sting, nor did the holy man stop from helping the scorpion, no matter what. The scorpion said, "I couldn't help myself, even though I might drown, I just had to sting you, I'm a scorpion after all."[6] The holy man is our sacred nature that never gives up on helping us whereas our egos are like the scorpion that doesn't consider the consequences of its actions but thinks only of satisfying immediate urges and desires.

In the grip of her ego obsession, Naomi couldn't help but to keep stinging herself. She also stung her husband and children, and would've stung me if I hadn't forced her to face the issue. She lied to herself and to her husband for years as she went deeper in debt. But, unlike the scorpion, this was not her true nature; her husband's love had awakened her Self

---

[6] Anandi Ma

and she found her way back.

Healthy Desire

Most of us seek to do or produce the best work we can. The desire to be the best at a trade or profession is a sign of psychological well-being. Our country was founded in part to avoid heavy taxation, which penalized those who excelled at their work. That laid the basis for the protestant work ethic that has been one of the governing principles of our lives. Our work ethic has made us the most prosperous country in the world, and we remain the leader in new and innovative technologies. Spiritual teachers have told us that work is important, and the fruits of labor are our just reward. Nowhere is this clearer than in the story from the New Testament:

A man going on a journey gathered his servants and gave them his goods. To one servant, he gave five talents, to another two, and to another one, to each according to their ability. Then the man went away. The servant who had five talents went at once and traded them, and made five talents more. So, also did he who had two talents. But, he who had one talent dug a hole in the ground and hid his master's money. Now after a long time, the master came home and called for his servants. And he who was given five talents said to his master "Here I have five talents more." His master said, "Well done, my good and faithful servant." And he also who had two talents came forward and delivered two more talents. The master said, "Well done, you have been faithful over a little, and I will give you much more." He who had received one talent came forward and said, "Master, I was afraid and so I buried your talent in the ground." The master answered him, "You slothful and wicked servant, you ought to have invested the talent. Take the talent and give it to him who has the ten talents."[7]

However, our culture's overemphasis on success and enjoying the fruits of hard work has elevated materialism over spirituality, instead of the reverse as in some Eastern cultures. From childhood onward, we are bombarded with messages that tell us happiness comes from material success. We idolize those people recognized for being successful whether in business, art, or the sports world. This is especially true of young people who all aspire to be the next Michael Jordan or Britney Spears. Tempering this rush to fame and fortune, we have the quiet voices of our ministers, teachers, and rabbis who remind us we are here to nurture and develop our whole self: body, mind, and spirit. The path of balance has been emphasized since the time of Confucius, who called it, "the golden mean;" the Buddha, "the middle way;" and Aristotle in his book of ethics, "the doctrine of the mean." For every course of action, we must avoid the two extremes of "excess" and "deficiency." Virtue, the right and middle course of action, lies between these two extremes.

My office is not far from that bastion of high-tech, Silicon Valley. The computer industry draws talent from around the world and has one of the most lucrative sub-economies in the country. It is the center of technological creativity and innovation. In spite of its leadership in these areas, this industry frequently experiences boom and bust cycles more intense than other economies. Over the years I have counseled many who have held prestigious high-paying jobs, only to lose them during a bust cycle, or those who had

---

[7] *Holy Bible*. Matt. 25.14

invested large amounts of money in their start-up companies, only to see them fail and lose their life savings. Most of them had a lot of difficulty dealing with these challenges. The more important a material lifestyle was to them, the greater their suffering. On the other hand, I've counseled some who saw these downturns as an opportunity to spend more time with their families and get away from the pressures of Silicon Valley. They relocated and found a less stressful job elsewhere, or made important lifestyle changes to put everything into proper balance.

Healing Excess

Naomi was deeply influenced by her surroundings. She lived in an upscale neighborhood and always tried to be one up on her neighbors. She needed to have the best of everything from custom drapes to the sharpest car in her driveway. As I became further acquainted with Naomi, it soon became evident that she was attempting to fill the emptiness inside her. But all the riches of the material universe could never have filled that void. In light of Naomi's suffering and that of many others who experienced grief from overindulgence, I thought about Jesus' admonishment. His warning, to cast off a member of our body if it endangers our soul, should be taken to heart. (A modern update might include credit cards as an offending "member.") The hell Jesus spoke of could very well have been the wretched lives of Naomi and untold millions of others who became a victim of greed and other excesses. I think that many of these people would gladly have given up a finger, hand, or foot to escape their personal hell and have peace, joy, and communion with the divine. I asked this question of Mary, one of my patients, who had been struggling against chemical addiction for twenty years. Mary said that she would gladly have given a hand or foot to be cured years ago. She added that if others could break their obsession in this manner, you'd have a line of people a mile long.

Talk therapy usually isn't sufficient to help the obsessed individual. Behavior modification is the best approach because it tends to remove the obsessed from the opportunity to engage in destructive activities. In Naomi's case, she surrendered all her credit cards and checkbooks. She couldn't trust herself to spend moderately, so we removed the opportunity for self-indulgence. This may seem draconian but it works most of the time. Typically the patient and I decide on their opportunities to engage their obsession and remove them. We then set a rigid behavioral structure that keeps the individual away from temptation throughout their day. In Naomi's case she avoided all shopping centers and sidewalk boutiques, only going to grocery stores. And then she would only take the cash she needed for grocery shopping.

Mary fought an addiction to marijuana for twenty years and avoided people and places where she could be influenced to smoke. But she was concerned because a very good friend who was a habitual user was coming to town. We decided that it was best that Mary didn't go to her friend's motel and that she get a mutual acquaintance to chauffer her about. She restricted contact to home visits, a controlled environment. In Mary's case, we examined possible risk opportunities and developed strategies to avoid them. Obsessed people are like the scorpion in our story. They will sting themselves and others unless stopped from indulging themselves. As we make progress to modify a person's habits and lifestyle, I strongly recommend depth therapy to shed light on their obsession. Some individuals are satisfied with lifestyle changes and aren't interested in exploring any deeper. For those who wish further therapy, we next work to uncover the thinking patterns that create their urges to overindulge, and then we reprogram them.

The scorpion's sting is truly depictive of obsessions. An instinctual urge to seek gratification takes hold of the person and cerebral processes are subjected to the whims of the ego. Recovery from obsessions requires discontinuing the behavior. The urges diminish with time when they are not fed, although they can resurface at any time. This is true no matter what the nature of the obsession. The individual is usually aware that their habit is self-destructive, but can't stop it. The help of a therapist, a self-help group, a twelve-step program, or a combination of these strategies is needed to break the obsession.

The Brothel and the Chapel

Once there were two friends walking down the street who came upon a crowd outside a chapel listening to a reading of scripture. "Come friend," said one to the other, "let us hear the sacred book." So saying the first man went inside and sat down. The second man peeped in but walked away. Presently he came across a house of ill repute. Immediately visions of delight took hold of him and he couldn't resist the urge to enter. Soon he felt disgusted with this place. "Shame on me!" he said to himself. "My friend has been listening to the holy word and sees where I am!" But the friend who was listening to the scriptures became bored and said, "What a fool I am! I have been listening to this boring book, when my friend is probably down the street at the house of ill repute having a great time." Later that night the two met up but they were killed in an auto accident. The messenger of death came for the soul of the one who had listened to the scriptures and dragged him off to hell. The messenger of God came for the second fellow who had been remorseful in the house of prostitution and led him up to heaven.[8]

As applied to our obsessions, what is the greater offense? To abstain from engaging in obsessive behavior but to wish otherwise, or to indulge oneself but be remorseful? It's not so much that unresolved issues drive us to such behavior, but that we recognize the obsession and seek therapy or spiritual help to remedy it. This reminds me of the story from the last chapter, *The Sannyasi's Lady of Ill Repute*, about the holy man whose body was in the temple but whose mind was always focused on the remorseful prostitute. We know which of them got to heaven. In this regard, the story of Tom's struggle with pornography comes to mind.

The Executive of Porn

Tom was a successful businessman, apparently happily married to Jane who worked in a jewelry store. Together they made a good living and enjoyed an upscale lifestyle. They vacationed two weeks in Hawaii every summer, skied at Vail in the winter, and relaxed on weekends at home, outings to San Francisco, or tours of the wine country. Everything appeared well adjusted on the surface. When Tom walked into the office, his aura of success and even-mannered demeanor had me wondering what could possibly be the problem. Looks can be deceiving. When Tom began to tell his story, I soon learned that a secret compulsion was

---

[8] *Tales and Parables of Sri Ramakrishna.* P.71 Sri Ramakrishna Math. Chennai. 2004

jeopardizing his happy marriage and affluent lifestyle.

Tom began, "Don, I'm addicted to pornography and I can't conceal it from my wife or my office staff much longer. Last Monday I was viewing a porn site in my office and getting aroused, when my secretary walked in and asked if I was okay, because my face was red and I looked different. Thank God that she didn't see what I was doing. I called and set this appointment the next day."

I said, "That's pretty high-risk behavior. Do you think you want to get caught?"

This idea startled him. "You know, maybe. I'm having more and more close calls, and it's just a matter of time, I guess."

"The part of you that wants to quit is forcing the issue," I said. He thought about this idea. "What do you think your wife would say?"

Tom shook his head in bewilderment. "She would really lose it—think I don't love her, or that I'm a pervert. She just wouldn't understand. I don't think I do," he said and looked at me for an answer.

"Tom, that will take therapy. But, in the short term, we need to modify your behavior, slow the impulse time to acting out for more conscious control so you don't get caught and we have time to sort through this." We decided to have him throw out all his porno magazines and books, to work on his home computer with its Internet access only when his wife was around. At the office, the plan was to have the door to his secretary's office open whenever he was working on his computer.

I could see that he was going to be a real struggle, that this obsession had a strong hold on him. I expected that we might have some setbacks. Things went reasonably well for the first few weeks, until one day he walked into my office in a state of panic. He told me that he had found a porn magazine hidden at his house last night, and drove to the dumpster at the local supermarket to throw it out. But this had ignited his compulsion. On the drive home, he turned around and went back to the dumpster and started looking for the magazine. As he was leaning into the dumpster, in a suit and tie, a car pulled up with its headlights on, and a man got out and approached him. Tom was in an absolute panic until the man asked for directions. What if it had been a policeman? He closed the hatch on the dumpster, stepped over, and directed the man to his restaurant.

This was the turning point; Tom said he was ready for more drastic intervention. Following our meeting, he swallowed his pride and enrolled in SAA (Sex Addicts Anonymous). He had friends who swore by SAA, and Tom was willing to give this a try in his desperation. This latest brush with exposure was so frightening that he began to attend the biweekly meetings religiously. Soon after, whenever the urge to indulge his obsession with porno arose, he was able to say a prayer, turn his will over to a higher power, and jump the hurdle. The support group helped, as did our weekly sessions, and Tom gathered the strength to work through his addiction

The best strategy to deal with an obsession is to structure a person's life so their chance for engaging in their obsessive behavior is minimized. This strategy worked well for Naomi, Mary, and Tom, and is the therapy of choice. I strongly recommend support groups such as the one Tom found helpful. I learned from Tom that SAA requires each person to set what they call a bottom line. This represents the point at which a person is likely to engage in the activity he is seeking to control. Addicts must draw a line one step above that activity to protect themselves from slipping into the obsession. In Tom's case, culture constantly exposes him to nudity. Magazines, newspapers, movies, the Internet, and all media feature immodest dress or behavior. It would have been impossible for him to stop reading, viewing, and exposing himself to pictures that might trigger his obsession. Tom decided to set up what he called a five-second rule for his bottom line. Whenever he saw a picture that might trigger his urge to indulge in pornography, he would take his mind off the picture within five seconds. As you recall, Mary refused to visit her friend at her hotel room. Naomi never carried credit cards or checkbooks when she left the house.

Tom was like the man in the brothel. While he was engaging in his loathsome activity, he really didn't want to participate. Tom attended two recovery groups for sex addiction. One group met weekly, and the second was an online network. He liked the online group because there was a lot of messaging back and forth. In a few months he was appointed their scribe, the individual in charge of messaging. Tom began to read the Bible and was able to distill the essential message of relevant passages and relate them to his group's struggles. He received much acknowledgment and support for his contribution. I met with Tom for several years, and in that time I witnessed a rather remarkable transformation. He became compassionate with himself and those who had similar obsessions, and this feeling began to extend to all people who suffered. His attitude at work changed, and he better managed his workers. He found peace reading biblical passages and letting his spirit soak up their meaning.

Communion with the Divine

A few months ago I was at a retreat with Shri Anandi Ma. One of the students asked Ma why she spends lengthy periods of time in silence and spiritual discipline. She said that anyone can slowly slip away from God, no matter how intimate their relationship. She said that as long as we have an ego anything is possible. This is why she stresses that we take time each day to meditate, pray, read scripture, or engage the sacred in a way meaningful to us. We not only lose a precious day of our lives without consciously touching the sacred; we also protect ourselves from succumbing to the temptations of the ego. My experience has born out this truth. For years I've made it a practice every morning to meditate, chant, or do both. Each day's experience is slightly different, but the most common is a communion of pure love with God, bestowing a peace and stillness that I can't describe, and the yearning to do God's will in my life.

My meditations were not always this sublime. I started meditating thirty years ago. During that period I've tried various practices and incorporated different spiritual disciplines. About fifteen years ago, I realized that I needed a teacher to help me progress. I prayed and asked for a teacher to help me deepen my spiritual practice. One day I attended an open meditation with Shri Anandi Ma given in Santa Cruz. It was remarkable. She was definitely the one. To strengthen the connection between us, I initially had many very deep and profound experiences the first few years, some of which have not repeated themselves again. Some experiences that always stayed with me were ones where I needed to make a decision or choice. If I stopped thinking about right or wrong, or whether or not to take an action, a little white light would appear between my eyes low on the forehead. This occurred every time I truly let the results of a decision go. I discovered much later that the light guiding my decisions was a light from my soul, and other people also had the same experiences. This small gift of spirit allowed me to relax about the outcome of a choice, knowing I was guided by a deep wisdom. Nevertheless, as most special experiences fell away, I felt a sense of boredom and duty creep into my morning practices. Some meditations were enriching, but others felt like a waste of time. This type of ennui is common for many meditative individuals and is one reason they discontinue.

For a few years, I became irregular in my morning practices, although I renewed contact with my guru whenever I could, here or in India. However, at subtle levels of the unconscious mind, a deepening effect was occurring that eventually reached my conscious awareness and renewed my practice. I was now eager to meditate every morning. My experiences, which can change at any time, have been very profound since then. Today I don't dare miss an opportunity to touch the sacred within myself. I also encourage friends with irregular morning spiritual practices to continue with them; my history has shown that it often takes years for the subtle effects of meditation to reach the surface. These experiences have not only allowed me to go deep within myself, but they gave me additional protection from the allures of material excesses.

The Love Obsession

Our ego can run away with any desire. The pursuit of love is no exception. Vince was nearing retirement after many years working as an aircraft mechanic. He enjoyed a wide circle of friends and was an amateur jeweler. Vince had been divorced for many years and had dated a lot of women but never found the right partner. One day he told me very excitedly, "Don, I found the woman I'm going to marry."

I knew he had been seriously searching for years, and I wholeheartedly congratulated him. A short while later I was introduced to Kim. She lived with her grown daughter and was a schoolteacher. Kim was very attractive and friendly, but my first impression was that she was insecure. A few months passed, and Vince began to tell me some disquieting stories. If the two of them were walking down the street, and Kim thought that he had looked at another woman passing by, she would get furious with him. At dinner Vince had to be careful not to look around the dining room at other guests, or Kim would accuse him of trying to meet someone else. Vince was exasperated. He had to be careful of what he said or did around Kim, or she would become very jealous. He couldn't be himself and would take great pains to avoid anything that would upset her.

Kim's unwarranted jealousy became a serious burden to their relationship. Although Vince bought her gifts and made jewelry for her, nothing seemed to reduce her anxiety that he was a man on the prowl. Vince was smitten with Kim and regularly proclaimed his love for her, but she refused to trust him. This situation came to a head at a party where Kim accused him of flirting with another woman. He became very angry with her, and they left separately. After a few weeks, Vince tried to contact her but she wouldn't take his phone calls or return his email. The next week he went to her house and rang the doorbell, but she refused to answer the door. He left upset but came back the next day. He pleaded with her to come to the door but to no avail. When he returned a third time, Kim told him to leave or she would call the police. He was undeterred and returned, and she reported him to the police saying that Vince was harassing her. He couldn't understand her chilly behavior. He kept repeating to me that he only had the best of intentions. I told him that she wasn't seeing him or the situation clearly; Kim was obviously projecting past fears onto him and was unable to enter into a relationship with him. Vince refused to accept this explanation.

As it turned out he was doing much the same. It had been a long time since Vince had experienced real intimacy and affection in a relationship as he did early on with Kim. Despite her turndowns, he kept projecting his need onto the situation. Each rejection only triggered a greater urge for Vince to explain his intentions and want to be with her. Vince's obsession for Kim prevented him from seeing that he was enslaved by his desire and couldn't adjust to the reality of their situation. A restraining order was levied against him, which he ignored and continued to pester her. Finally they ended up in court. A sympathetic judge told Vince that any further infraction of his restraining order would mean a jail sentence. What started as a hopeful relationship between two adults took a very bad turn, fueled by Kim's projections and Vince's love obsession. His story reminds me of the barber in the following story.

The Jar of Desire Can Never be Filled

A barber was passing under a tree when a voice said, "Will you accept seven jars full of gold?" Looking about and seeing no one, he cried aloud, "Yes I shall accept the seven jars." At once came the reply, "Go home, I have carried the jars of gold to your house." The barber ran home in haste to verify the truth of this claim. When he entered his house, he saw to his complete and utter amazement seven jars before him. Delighted beyond belief, he opened each one and found six filled to the rim with gold and the seventh half-filled with gold. As his excitement abated, he realized his happiness was incomplete because he did not receive his full measure of gold as promised. A strong desire arose in him to fill the last jar to the rim with gold. He converted all his ornaments into a large heap of gold coins and put them into the jar, but the mysterious vessel was, as before, unfilled.

The barber was a favorite of the court, so he asked the king for an increase in his stipend. The king was very generous and gave the barber a handsome increase. The barber raced home and added the additional coins to the last jar, but it remained partly unfilled. He became more desperate, so he began starving himself and his family to save more cold coins to put in the jar. Finally he went door to door begging for food, which he sold for more coins, but the jar showed no signs of filling. Months passed and the barber grew more and more miserable. Finally the king asked him what was wrong.

"What is the matter with you? Did you not get the seven jars?"

Startled the barber said, "Your majesty how did you know I have seven jars? Who informed you of this?"

The king said, "Don't you know that this is the work of a demon trickster? He offered me the same seven jars, but I declined. No one can spend that much money. It only brings with it the desire of hoarding. Go at once and return the money, and you will feel well again."[9]

---

[9] Ibid. P.51

Vince had a taste from the jar and wanted more. Naomi was caught trying to fill hers. The jar of desire was inside both of them and could never be filled. The Buddha said craving begets craving. His solution was to recognize that all our suffering comes from desire, to avoid attachment to transitory pleasures, and to create a desire for that which is enduring and permanent. Then with discerning wisdom, we can make better choices in our lives. The jar of desire can only be permanently filled by divine love.

This doesn't mean that love is a trap or is to be avoided. My understanding of Vedanta's thinking on love is that the desire to love contains a ray of divine love, which finds its expression in loving partnership. To successfully integrate the spiritual into such a relationship, I believe we need to find a partner with an acceptable degree of spiritual compatibility. Next we need to cultivate the tools to work our way through the vicissitudes of human relationships. Most importantly our love should not be only for the physical form and characteristics of our partner, but seeing the deeper dimension of how they reflect the God and Goddess. Since illness and death are a part of life, we need to recognize that the physical form of our loved one will not be with us permanently. When our partner has passed on, we can carry their love in our heart and know that the divine part of them is eternal. Grief is a part of love but its excess only tarnishes the experience.

Rather it should lead us to seek a love of the divine reflected in them that is eternal and more complete. Our partnership will have given us a glimpse of divine love.

What society often considers love is frequently just infatuation, often with some part of us, an ideal, or a past love experience instantly projected onto another. Vince became infatuated with his own need to love and be loved, and he projected it onto Kim. It was a projection that had little to do with who Kim was as an individual, despite her own failings in the relationship. This became obvious when he persisted in his pursuit, despite her evident desire to break it off and in the face of a court order. She became an object for his projection, not a real person with her own feelings, needs, and rights. Vince's obsession with his needs and desires almost landed him in jail, and could've easily led to his ruin.

Consciousness Suffers

When the ego takes charge of our thinking, our mind and all its resources focus on obtaining the ego's goals, so we lower our consciousness. Our intellect becomes a tool of the ego. Rather than raising our consciousness, we place a ceiling on its functioning. We also lose sight of the God and Goddess in everyone we meet, and are unable to see that the Self in us is the same in them. We fail to scale the heights of consciousness and experience the Self as a perfect ray of the Absolute Consciousness. This is the pain that Maharishi Patanjali speaks of: "Ignorance is the view that the ephemeral, the impure, the pain of suffering—that which is not the Self—is permanent, pure, pleasurable, and the true Self . . . One of the prime causes of suffering is . . . ignorance of your True Self and the value of spirituality."[10]

I was sharing these ideas with Mary who gave me permission to use her real name in my book. Mary is fifty

---

[10] *Yoga Sutras of Patanjali*. 11.5 Stiles. Weiser Books, Cananda 2002

years old, has the map of Ireland written on her face, will laugh at the drop of a hat, and often takes herself too seriously. She has been in a stable but challenging relationship for twenty years and has fought marijuana addiction longer than that. When I met Mary, she was smoking daily but through various behavioral interventions and the help of twelve-step programs, she managed to stop her addiction. Mary showed a particular interest in the spiritual, and we talked at length on how she could weave this interest into her daily life. As she became clean and sober, she began reading the Bible whenever she was tempted to use drugs. Mary was successful for two or three months before she started smoking again. This time it was more difficult for her to quit than with previous attempts. The interventions and strategies we used the first time didn't work now. She felt miserable about her failure but couldn't give up her addiction. We had one conversation that proved to be a turning point for Mary. She told me that she didn't feel good reading the Bible, and while she did ask for spiritual help, Mary felt very distant from Jesus. She told me her prayers felt hollow and didn't have heartfelt energy.

I told Mary, "You're functioning now more like an animal than a human being, in that the energy you're putting out is at a very low vibration. Basically your thoughts are nothing more than a wave of energy vibrating at a certain frequency. When you think a thought, you're sending out a wave of energy at a given frequency. That's why friends who think alike tend to attract one another, and why the old saying 'water seeks its own level' carries so much truth. But when you're functioning at a primitive level, you will emit thought waves at a lower frequency.

"The gap between your consciousness now as to when you

were reading the Bible and helping others is quite different. Then you were emitting the much finer vibrations of compassion and love. God, as Supreme Consciousness, emits the finest and most refined vibrations in the universe. When your thoughts and feelings, generated by your activities and focus, are closer to that vibration then your prayers reach the Source faster and you tend to get that for which you ask. Now, however, your vibration is low and the opposite is true. In general, your healing will now require stronger intent, much more so than when your consciousness was more elevated. Our job on this planet, if you want to call it that, is to evolve our consciousness to its ultimate state and experience the divine in ourselves and throughout the whole of creation. My advice to you is to do everything we did before but with renewed vigor and in God's name to break your addiction. The good news is that once you get clean again, you will not have lost spiritual ground and can reclaim the level of awareness that you once had."

Mary stopped smoking pot shortly after we discussed these ideas. It wasn't long before she regained her former level of heightened awareness. On her free time, she found new compassionate pursuits. She is now helping others, currently looking for a volunteer advocacy position, and has added many spiritual and inspired books to her reading list along with the Bible.

Mary's experience underscores what can happen to us when we indulge our desires to excess, or in her particular case give in to our addictions. Not only do we suffer, but we cause those we love to suffer, as was the case with Naomi and Vince and surely with Tom if he hadn't stopped in time; but we also dehumanize ourselves and place a ceiling on our consciousness, which stops our personal evolution to the

Godhead. This is capsulated in verse by Sri Chaitanya, a 16th century Bhakti yoga ascetic, who encouraged personal experience of the divine:

Alas for those who spend their days
In festive mirth and joy:
The dazzling, deadly, liquid form
Their hearts for'er employ.

The shining bottles charm their eyes
And draws their heart's embrace;
The slaves of wine can never rise
From what we call disgrace.
Man's glory is in common sense
Dictating us thy grace;
That man is made to live and love
The beauteous Heaven's embrace.

The flesh is not our own alas;
The mortal frame a chain;
The soul confined for former wrongs
Should try to rise again.

Why then this childish play in that
Which cannot be our own;
Which falls within a hundred years
As if a rose a blown.

Enjoyment, sorrow, what but lots
To which the flesh is heir;
The soul that sleeps alone concludes
In them it has its share.

And then, my friends, no more enjoy
Nor weep for all below;
The women, wine and flesh of beasts
No love on thee bestow.

So push thy onward march, O soul,
Against an evil deed
That stands with soldiers Hate and Lust
A hero be indeed.

Maintain thy post in spirit world
As firmly as you can;
Let never matter push you down
O stand heroic man![11]

Sister De Sales' Prankster

When I was a student in Catholic grade school, the nuns were very strict. I used to get into a lot of trouble. Once I was caught gambling in the boy's bathroom. My mother was called to school. After I received a tongue lashing from Sister De Sales, the school principle, I got another kind of lashing from my mother. I didn't see anything wrong with pitching pennies against the wall and continued it elsewhere. Another time I threw a kid in the garbage bin; he had a panic attack and I found myself in Sister De Sales' office again, and my mother was once again told how terrible I was. I had been thrown in the same bin many times and came out laughing

[11] Sri Chaitanya. Srila Bhakativinode, *Saragrahi Vaishnava "1874"* San Rafael, CA 2001

and smelling like spoiled lunchmeat. I couldn't understand why this kid freaked out. One time in 5th grade, friends and I went on strike with picket signs demanding shorter class periods and longer lunches. It was a prank, but the nuns didn't see it that way, and I was suspended for the rest of the week.

A particular problem for me was that my brother was the teacher's pet. He was three years younger and a straight A student, and I couldn't compete with him academically. I had trouble paying attention, let alone getting good grades. When report cards were handed out, the priest would call me to the front of the class, announce how well my brother did, and then take a ruler to my knuckles. I would be sick to my stomach waiting for my turn with the ruler. At the time it seemed like being good their way was too difficult. I couldn't get it right. By the time I left eighth grade, I gave odds on the devil possessing my soul. About that time, I became aware of girls and the devil could have had me for a penny. I thought that religion and morality were for others, and I was somehow different. I wanted to be good but just couldn't quite meet their definition of that term. Unbeknownst to me, a solid spiritual groundwork had been laid down just beneath my conscious awareness. I wouldn't discover that until later in life.

When I reflect back on my life and the various hats I've worn—naval officer, stock broker, therapist, and writer—I know that at each stage the opportunity to get trapped in excess was always present. As a naval officer, I drank too much. As a stockbroker, I didn't always put my client's interest first. When my first marriage ended, I was really lost and sought to fill myself through brief romantic interludes. But I never took any of these activities to an extreme;

something inside, some guiding light always brought me back to an even keel. I see now that it was my Self or Soul leading me to the divine on my own path at my own pace. I don't believe my personal experiences were much different from other people's lives. I am all too human. I was exactly like the man in the story who sat in the house of ill repute while wishing he wasn't there. But after what some would call my religious conversion, and I would call my spiritual awakening, I began to experience the sacred manifested in ways I never would have dreamed possible years ago. This happened because I kept trying, despite fallbacks, to keep on this track.

As I read the New Testament, I am deeply touched by what Jesus was purported to have said. His love and compassion for man was so great that it comes through even in the most demanding passages. His heart bled for those around Him. He told them the only law was the law of love. He knew all too well man's frailties and man's ability to turn what is good into something loathsome. Jesus told those who would judge themselves superior to look at themselves more closely. He told those who would put themselves first, that they would actually be last. He walked and ate with adulteresses and prostitutes. He stood beside those that had slipped into excesses. Jesus understood we are all too human. I know He would have laughed at my childhood escapades. I know He was there watching over me when the wild horses of my desires took the reins from my hands.

We are fragile. The perennial teachings guide us so that we can discover our true nature. We can't do it alone. The job is too big. We need to call on spiritual resources that are meaningful to us in the culture and epoch in which we live. All teachers through the ages have told us as much.

"Children, how hard it is to enter the kingdom of God? It

is easier for a camel to go through the eye of a needle than for a rich man to enter the kingdom of God." And they were exceedingly astonished, and said to Him, "Then who can be saved?" Jesus looked at them and said, "With men it is impossible, but not with God; for all things are possible with God."[12]

Life seeks our evolution and will give us many opportunities to redirect ourselves. Our urges and passions may run us for a while and then we hurt ourselves. Each time that happens, the opportunity is ripe to ponder our life and make new choices. Sooner or later most of us realize that we are caught in destructive behavior that leads us to emptiness and futility. It is then that we are reminded of the sage's advice.

"There are five primal causes of suffering: ignorance of your True Self, *the value of spirituality; egoism* and its self centeredness; *attachment to pleasure*; aversion to pain; and clinging to life out of fear of death."[13]

The jar of desire can never be filled. The ghost of greed can't be stopped and the scorpion stings itself. These tales are reminders to rule our lives from the Self. Ego inflation and ego deflation are the demons inside us. Obsessions are trickster demons, and while they appear as friends here to help us, they turn against us when we are least aware.

Man's glory is in common sense
Dictating us thy grace;
That man is made to live and love

---

[12] *Holy Bible*. Mark 24
[13] *Yoga Sutras of Patanjali*, bid.

The beauteous Heaven's embrace.
Maintain thy post in spirit world
As firmly as you can;
Let never matter push you down,
O stand heroic man![14]

---

[14] Sri Chaitanya. Srila Bhakativinode, P.71 *Saragrahi Vishnava "1874"* San Rafael, CA 2000

Chapter Seven
Raising Consciousness

A great king meandered into a forest one day and came upon a sage. He talked with the sage and was very impressed with his purity of thought and wisdom, so the king invited the sage to his castle. The king wanted to oblige the sage and offered him a gift, which the sage refused. Upon being question by the king, the sage said, "I am a simple man, the fruits of the forest and its waters are sufficient for me. Why should I take a present from you my good lord?"

The king said, "Just to benefit me sir, please take something from my hands, anything that pleases you." The sage continued to refuse any gift from the king. That night the king prayed to God repeatedly, "Lord, give me more children. Lord, give me more wealth. Lord, give me more territory. Lord, keep my body in good health, and so he prayed throughout the night. The next morning the sage happened to see the king in prayer and quickly left the room. When the king saw him, he ran after the sage crying out,

"Don't leave yet, you have not taken my gift. Please accept my gift."

The sage turned abruptly and said to the king, "I do not beg of beggars. You yourself are a beggar. You cannot trick God by offering me gifts while seeking to be dishonest with yourself. Do you take me for a fool?"[1]

The Pitfalls

The ancient temple in Delphi circa 300 B.C. had inscribed on it, "Know the truth, for the truth shall set you free." This freedom will come to us as we discover our true nature and the true purpose of our incarnation on planet earth. In India sages speak of two paths to the divine. One is the path of the wandering renunciant, the sadu, who only has a loincloth and begging bowl. Society takes care of him as he moves about on his holy business. The other is the path of the householder. That is our path. The householder must have all the resources of the ego, not only to survive but to explore the depths of his soul.

Many times the path to the Self requires us to do the opposite of our natural inclinations. Jesus' teaching to "turn the cheek" is just one example of the sometimes puzzling and elusive nature of the quest for truth. We are told not to feel hurt when someone critiques us, to depersonalize their criticism. It appears that proper action is to swallow our pride in this case in order to make progress in knowing our true selves. The Katha Upanishad written two thousand years ago helps us towards this progress:

---

[1]   Vivekananda. *The Yoga & Other Works*. 445. Ramakrishna/Vivekananda Center. N.Y., N.Y 1984

"God made man turn outward; man therefore looks outward, not into himself. Now and again, a daring soul, desiring immortality, has looked back and found God within himself."[2]

We may try with willpower to raise our consciousness, but unless we avoid the tendencies of our conditioning, we are going to get stuck in emotional mire. The most frequent pitfalls I have come across in my own search and in my therapy practice with patients is the subject of this chapter. They are not major revelations about us or mysterious aspects of our mind, but simple inherent tendencies that we act on every day and that hold us at a surface level of consciousness. I took this list from the ego defense mechanism rediscovered by modern psychology, since sages in their own languages have been pointing them out for ages:

A. self deception (either denial or repression)
B. judgment (a critical form of projection)
C. projection (unconsciously thinking our thoughts are what the other person thinks, believes or feels)
D. personalization (not a true defense mechanism, but an enormous challenge)

What I find interesting is that on one hand these reactive defenses block entrance to the transcendent, but once known and acknowledged they become guideposts that show us where we are on our path to self-realization. More than that,

---

[2]   Purhit, Swami, & Yeats, Y.B. *The Ten Principle Upanishads*. Katha Upanishad. Farber & Farber. London 1985

each time we become aware of their operation, we witness the functioning of our mind and experience presence. This presence only appears when we are fully focused and aware in the present moment. There is no thought of the past or future. This is beingness without thought. This is the Witness Consciousness of the stilled mind and ego. Therefore it is an experience of the eternal Self, and it is this consciousness that continues when we shed our bodies.

The Buddha Said
"More than those who hate you,
more than all your enemies,
an undisciplined mind does greater harm.
More than your mother,
more than your father,
more than all your family,
a well trained mind
a well disciplined mind does greater good."[3]

The Buddha says it is our task to make the mind work for us and not against us; or, in the words of an ancient sage, "To turn inward, not outward, to find our soul." For that we need the ego as a kind of wounded guide to show us our progress along the path.

Self Deception
The first pitfall is not being brutally honest with ourselves, as we see from the Beggar King story. We can kid ourselves

---

[3] Easwaran, Ekanath. *The Dammapada.* Mind. Nilgiri Press. Canada 2007

by acknowledging some of the truths we know about our behavior but deny some of the most troublesome aspects. In Chapter One we discussed the need to be totally clear about our perception of reality to avoid seeing life through distorted lenses. The more we experienced reality without these distortions the more we activated our higher functioning. We must possess this complete and thorough honesty to know ourselves and follow the path of our true selves.

Julian Tries to Fool Himself

Julian shuffled into my office one day complaining about his father again. Julian was twenty years old, worked part time at a tech store, and took a few classes at a local college. He started by saying, "Don, my father doesn't respect me."

"Give me an example of what you mean."

"It's just the way he treats me; he talks down to me all the time, tells me to do things for him like I was a little kid, and mostly dismisses anything I say."

I had been working with Julian for a year and knew a lot about his irresponsible lifestyle and his diffident attitude about everything. I thought it was time to be blunt with him. I said, "Julian, you have to earn respect. You took three classes this semester and dropped two of them, even though you're an A student. You come home to your parent's house at four in the morning stoned; you won't help around the house. You treat yourself and your parents like crap, and you want respect. It won't happen until you respect yourself."

Julian was startled for a moment, and then angrily spit out. "Well, I think you're full of it. My friends treat me with respect, even if you and my dad don't."

"Most of your friends are like you; they live off their parents and smoke a lot of dope. 'Birds of the feather stick together,' as they say. All of you should be getting on with your lives, I mean, do you really respect them, do they really respect you?" Julian didn't have a ready answer. He thought about it, fidgeted, looked away, and then laughed.

Finally he said, "Damn it, what's so bad about wanting to party at my age? I have plenty of time to be responsible like my parents. I don't want to look back twenty years from now and have regrets."

"I have clients in their thirties who can't hold a job, can't commit to a relationship, telling me the same thing." Julian looked back at me in alarm. A light went on somewhere inside of him. "But, that's not the issue here," I added. "You're acting irresponsibly and no one respects that. If you were living at home, going to college full time with the goal of being self-sufficient at some point, your father's attitude would change. But, you'd rather live off him and act like a fifteen year old. You know it's not right. You don't respect yourself and your dad is simply reflecting that back to you, and you blame him for doing it. Psychologists call that projection, because you project your feelings onto your father. On top of that, you really don't respect your friends deep down, yet you use them to excuse your own immature behavior."

Julian stood up and began to walk around the room. "Okay, okay. I get it."

"I'll just make one more point. Unlike your friends, you are beginning to notice that reflection. Life is showing you it's time to grow up and stop blaming others for your own immaturity. Partying and smoking dope is just a cover-up for not owning up to it." I laughed. "The problem, Julian, is that you're too self-aware, and you can't get away with it anymore. The messaging back to you will only get more pointed over time. It has been said that life is a mirror, and people like you validate that truism."

Julian came back around and sat down in his chair. He got the message, it seemed. "So, you think I should take a full load of courses next semester?"

"I think you should decide on a course of study that excites you, and then go for it." He began to think about that. In the next few sessions we discussed what he really wanted to do with his life. What really excited him was working with computers, but he didn't want to be a "geek."

"Oh, you mean like Steve Jobs."

"No. He's really cool." Julian got the message. It's not what you do, but it's who you are. He was finally on his way.

Julian knew at some level that he was fooling himself. His deception may appear obvious to us as adults, but we fall into the same trap as Julian when we are dishonest with ourselves. Sometimes our subterfuge may be subtle and we may not catch it at all. We need to be ever vigilant and become a witness of our own behavior if we are to use it as a path to self-transcendence.

A Saint Mourns His Critic

There was a saint in India whose evening gatherings with his disciples were often disrupted by a skeptical neighbor who found fault with everything the saint said or did. The disciples wanted to throw him out but the master would not hear of it. One evening a disciple appeared at the evening discussion reporting with a broad smile. "Master," he cried exultantly, "your enemy, the critic, is dead!"

"Ah, alas!" cried the saint, tears welling up in his eyes. "I am heartbroken. My best friend has left behind this world. He was the only one who was willing to help me by pointing out my faults. Shall I ever find another as true to my well-being as he?"[4]

Like most people, I can't say that I wholeheartedly welcome criticism. I was often criticized as a child and never quite met the expectations of my parents and teachers. When my parents wanted to talk to me about something, I knew that 'something' wasn't a compliment. To some degree, I have that same knee-jerk reaction to criticism today, in spite of working on myself over the years. If I am prepared for negative feedback, I am okay with it, but if I get caught off guard, I constantly have to re-center myself.

Welcome or not, feedback often allows us to recognize parts of our self that we have not fully owned or don't like to examine. In spite of brief feelings of apprehension, most of us want to confront and overcome our faults. With awareness and constant practice, it becomes easier for us to accept feedback and sift through it to find the gems. Many of my clients work diligently in this way and experience greater ease and facility in self-examination, more so than they thought possible at first.

Judgment

Judging others is another trap that keeps us at the ego level. We pull away from God with such judgments because we are subtly or unknowingly enhancing our egos by putting ourselves in a superior position. The superior/inferior attitude inherent in judgment prevents us from acknowledging ourselves and accepting our brothers and sisters as individualized units of God consciousness, no

---

[4] Story, Anandi Ma

higher and no lower. Judgment is a major block to discovering the Self.

A Yogi Learns Humility

A yogi returned from the forest having spent many years engaged in meditation and other spiritual practices. Prior to leaving the forest, he had an experience of his spiritual powers that left him in awe. As he was about to leave, a few leaves fell on his head. He looked up and saw a crow and a crane fighting on the top branches of the tree, which made him very angry. He knew this was a sign of worldliness, and in a fit of anger said, "How dare you throw these leaves on my head." Saying it, a lightening bolt like a flash of anger went out from him and burnt the birds to ashes. Astonished by his new yogic powers, he set off for town. After a while he came to a house and knocked on a door and asked for some bread, as was the custom of yogis who depended on the goodness of others for their sustenance. At the door he cried out, "Mother, give me some food."

A voice from inside said, "Wait a little my son."

The young man thought: 'You wretched woman, how dare you make me wait? You do not know of my powers.'

While he was thinking these thoughts, the voice said, "Boy, do not be thinking too much of yourself. Here is neither crow nor crane." He was astonished, but still he had to wait.

At last the woman came, and he humbly asked her, "Mother, how did you know about the birds?"

She said, "My boy, I do not know your yoga or other such practices. I am a simple woman. I made you wait because my husband is ill and I was nursing him. I just struggle to do my duty. But by minding my business and doing the simple things God has set for me, I have become illumined and thus I could read your thoughts and know what you had done in the forest." Feeling sorry for the young man and believing he had learned a lesson, she told him if he wanted to know higher truths he should visit a certain man in the village. Alarmed that she would send him to an avydha (one belonging to the lowest caste), he declined. The next day, thinking about his recent experience with the simple woman, he decided that he might learn something from a man of humble origin. He found the man, a big avydha with a big knife cutting meat. 'Lord help me,' he thought, 'is this the man I am going to learn from? He is the incarnation of a demon.'

In the meantime, the man looked up and said, "O Swami, did a lady send you here?" The Yogi nodded his head. "Take a seat until I am done with my business." The butcher finished his work and took the yogi home with him. He then said, "Sir, sit here," and went into the house. He then bathed his father and mother, fed them, and did all he could to please them, after which he went out to the swami. "Now sir, you have come to see me. What can I do for you?" The yogi asked him a few questions about the soul and God, and then the avydha gave him a lecture from the Mahabharata, which contains some of the loftiest doctrines of Vedanta.

When the avydha finished, the young man asked, "Why are you in that terrible body and doing such ugly work?"

The avydha answered, "I am not a yogi and have no special powers. I just do my duty. My mind is not cluttered with other things. All my knowledge comes to me from God, simple as I am. I do not judge, I do not complain, I am simply an unlearned man with knowledge of truth."[5]

The yogi left the avydha ashamed of himself. He vowed never to judge anyone again. He began to teach all who came to him simplicity and humbleness. Never again did he use his yogic powers.

Humility is a great cure for judgment. If we can learn to say to ourselves, "Who am I to judge?" we may overcome this tendency to criticize others rather than looking at our self.

> Seeking blemishes in others
> Those who laugh and sarcasm tend,
> They ignore their own blemishes
> Which have no beginning or end.
> Near thee keep a vitup'rator,
>
> In thy courtyard erect him a hut,
> He washes thee sparkling clean
> Without soap and without water.
> Don't distance a vitup'rator,
> Rather give him respect and honor;
> He keeps thy body and heart clean
> Exaggerating faults of others.
> Don't extol thyself so as to
> Nickname others paltry and vain,
> Nobody knows under which tree
> A bone the garbage may contain.[6]

---

[5] *The Yoga & Other Works*. Ibid. p.480.
[6] Mohan Singh Karki, *Kabir* Motilal Banarsidass Pub. Private Ltd. Delhi

Kabir writes that others reflect our behavior, "seeking blemishes in others . . . ignore their own blemishes" and, "don't nickname other paltry and vain, nobody knows under which tree a bone the garbage may contain." Second, he advises using the vituperator's criticism to become aware of one's own shortcomings. The second suggestion is particularly difficult to implement. Most of us tend to respond to criticism defensively as Julian was prone to do. It is more difficult and more rewarding to emulate the saint who used his critic to know himself.

Judging others and projecting the contents of our minds onto them are two ego defenses that work hand in hand as was the case with Mimi.

Mimi's Criticism of the President

Mimi said, "Don, there's another experience I want to share that bears out what you've told me the previous week. I was avoiding my boyfriend, upset that he wasn't giving me the type of support I needed. One morning in meditation, I realized that he was doing his best even though it didn't meet my particular needs at the time. When I realized this, I stopped being critical of him and felt sorry for the trouble I caused him." Mimi went on to say that she was now able to appreciate his wonderful qualities, and that these insights came from a place of quiet within her.

I told her, "You're sharing some great insights with me on how we unconsciously judge others when they don't meet our needs, but do you want to stretch yourself a little more?"

"Sure," she said.

"Okay, I know you really dislike President Bush. Will you please tell me why you are so angry with him? When you talk about him, you get all upset."

"He's stupid, got us into a lot of trouble, and he won't listen to anybody; it's his way or the highway."

I asked her if she could apply what we just talked about to him. She said that she had no idea how to do that. I added, "Mimi, your emotions are clouding your vision, so let me help you. Would you say it's fair to call the president very rigid?"

"Yes, most definitely," she replied

"Would you say he refuses to listen to advice?"

"Yes, from those outside his inner circle."

I said, "Would you say he appears stubborn?" She nodded her head emphatically. I asked her, "Okay, Mimi, who in your own family acts that way?"

She thought about it for a moment. "I was raised by a father who is obsessive compulsive, and a mother who demanded that everything be exact."

"Good, but a few sessions ago, you told me your grandparents were early pioneers and established a very successful business by running it with an iron fist and smashing the competition. You had to dress and speak a certain way, or they would criticize you. You were unable to reason with either your parents or grandparents, and had to live under the iron fist with both of them."

Mimi said, "Oh my God, you're absolutely right. The qualities I hate in the president are the same attitudes that my family tormented me with as a child."

"Very good," I said. "Now can you see that the president is caught in his own pattern of rigidity, losing some of his political support because he can't save the world with an inflexible approach to complex problems?" Mimi tentatively nodded her head.

Mimi was able to understand how she created her personal

world. She had to push beyond the constraints of her emotions and 'grind her teeth,' as Vasistha, Rama's teacher, once counseled.

"The highest state of consciousness can be attained by all, even primitive men, for it involves only the rise of wisdom . . . . Abandon your reliance on fate or gods created by dull-witted people and by self-effort and self-knowledge make the mind non-mind. Let the infinite mind swallow, as it were, the finite mind and go beyond everything . . . .In this world, anger and emotion impels man to do what should not be done, but tranquility enables one to do what should be done. Do not give way to emotion or anger; that is surely the path to disaster. For, what will be will be. Each individual sees only those objects that are rooted in his own mind, it is only because of the forgetfulness of truth that confusion arises . . . True dispassion does not arise in one by austerity, charity, pilgrimage, etc. but only by directly perceiving one's own nature. Hence with intense right self-exertion and grinding one's teeth . . . one will cultivate the ability to see the truth."[7]

As the Buddha said,

"More than those who hate you,
more than all your enemies,
an undisciplined mind does greater harm.
More than your mother,
more than your father,
more than all your family,

---

[7] Venkatesananda, Swami. *Vassistha's Yogi*. 111:112, 1V:11 State University of N.Y. Press 1993

a well trained mind
a well disciplined mind does greater good."[8]

It's clear that Mimi was not only judging the president for his performance in office, but that she was also projecting her unresolved family issues onto him. She had an "ah hah" revelation about herself when she stopped judging and projecting. That allowed her to dredge up and become aware of a host of buried emotions. Earlier I said that the ego serves us by letting us know about ourselves. In Mimi's case, once she saw how her ego criticizes others, an alarm began to sound. It doesn't sound all the time now, but it does sound quite frequently.

Projection

We have delved into the tendency for us to project our thoughts onto the world and call it reality. The problem with projection is that we look outside ourselves and not inside, where we are out of harmony with truth of our beingness. Even the most evolved amongst us need be watchful of projection, as the sadu in the following classic story learned to his humiliation.

The Sadhu and the Goddess

Two sadhus, who were very advanced in their spiritual practices, were trekking across India. They had long since given up a material way of life and the desires that are a part of that existence. One morning they came to a river that had

---

[8] *The Dammapada*. Ibid. Mind

swollen to its banks from a recent storm. They were about to place their small bags on their heads and walk across the river when they heard a voice downstream. Being in no hurry, they walked down and found a beautiful young woman in distress because she couldn't cross the stream. The sadhus had taken a vow of chastity and had never even talked to a young woman, let alone been this close to one. Immediately one of the sadhus put his small cloth on the ground, picked up the woman, and forged the river with her clinging to his arms. When he reached the other side, he put her down; she went on her way, and the two companions continued on their trek. Several hours later, as they sat down for their midday meal, one of the men appeared very upset. His partner asked him if he was getting ill. His companion replied, "You carried that young woman across the river and broke your vows, how could you do such a thing?"

His partner said, "I didn't see a young woman; I saw the Goddess and helped her forge the river. As soon as I put her down, I thought no more of her and my mind was elsewhere. You my dear friend, however, continue to carry a young woman in your head and you have not yet put her down."[9]

This is a theme, dwelling on images or thoughts and not releasing them, that has popped up in several earlier stories. Here, it appears with a new twist or understanding of how the mind works. The sadhu who was critical of his companion was actually accusing him of his own preoccupation with the young woman. He projected his ego thinking onto his friend who was in a state of non-dual consciousness. The enlightened sadhu acted as a mirror reflecting back to his

---

[9] Story, Shri Anandi Ma

critic the contents of his projected thoughts.

If the critical sadhu had been aware of psychological projection, he would have realized that he was only reflecting his own thinking rather than being a mind reader. Being upset with his friend should have been a clue that he was actually judging himself for entertaining such thoughts. If he had been more detached and spiritually or psychologically astute, he would have worked to resolve his own issues with women, which was the cause of his distress. He didn't understand that other people often reflect back to us our unwelcome shadow projections so that we can objectively see them.

Personalization

As I mentioned earlier, one of my most difficult challenges is that of being too sensitive to what others say about me. I am not alone. In my practice, my clients are constantly challenged not to react to demeaning and abusive comments from others—their mate or from co-workers or their boss— who make uninformed emotional judgments about them.

We all live in our own little universe; that is, we perceive the world through the filter of our senses. Since none of us is a replica of the other, we will have a different perspective and different opinions about what is actually occurring in any given situation. Through the ego process of projection, unless a person is completely centered, they will color what they say to us. When we take offense to what is being said, we personalize their comments and cause ourselves distress.

The Four Agreements, written by Don Miguel Ruiz, teaches Toltec wisdom from an ancient Mesoamerican tradition. The second of four agreements is, don't take anything personally.

"Nothing people do is because of you. It is because of themselves. All people live in their own dream, in their own mind; they are in

a completely different world from the one we live in. When we take something personally, we make the assumption that they know what is in our world, and we try to impose our world on their world...Even when a situation seems so personal, even if others insult you directly, it has nothing to do with you. What they say and do, and the opinions they give are according to the agreements they have in their own minds. Their point of view comes from all the programming they received during domestication."[10]

It is important to remember that others act as our mirrors, reflecting back what we have unresolved within ourselves. Our task is to sift through what is being said for useful feedback that can help us become aware and centered in our lives and see through the defenses of our ego.

The Saint Who Was Spat On

There's a story of a saint who went to bathe in the river, and after he came out, someone spat on him. So, without getting angry, he went again and bathed, and again came out. This happened one hundred times.

This person was hired by someone else to make this saint angry. Finally he became very frustrated, saying, "I have spat on this person a hundred times, and without getting angry, he very coolly and calmly goes back into the river and then comes out again." Then the man fell at the saint's feet, saying, "I'm sorry, but someone hired me to do this."

The saint answered, "Why didn't you tell me in the first place? I would have exhibited being very angry and you

---

[10] Ruiz, don Miguel. *The Four Agreements*. The Second Agreement. Amber Allen Pub. San Raphael, CA 1997

wouldn't have had the trouble of spitting on me a hundred times. But in spite of that, thank you very much. Thank you so much for doing it, because I had the opportunity to bathe a hundred times in this holy river and much of my negative karma was washed away. So indeed you are a great being."[11]

This story may appear unrealistic and the saint's virtue unattainable. It is not. I have known teachers who have attained that stage of consciousness. The guru of my guru, Shri Dhyanyogi, was such a saint. He said he wanted to populate the earth with minions who would teach as he did. We start where we are. It doesn't matter if we are hypersensitive or not. The source within us is infinite and has infinite potential. We need only to start down the path.

Personalizing what others say about us creates an emotional reaction. We lose our objectivity and experience life through a distorted prism. It is difficult, if not impossible, to solve challenges when we are not rational. Perhaps in intimate relationships, more than any other type of relationships, our buttons get pushed. Personal relationships can be a crucible for growth and awareness, or cause a reaction and smallness of being to hide beneath.

Bob and Jenny's Dance of Blame

Pointing a finger at her husband, Bob, Jenny said to me through her tears, "I just want to get a divorce; I can't stand my husband. He won't talk to me, he hardly says hello, he ignores me when I talk to him, and he acts as if I'm not there." Bob sat quietly as she ranted on about him. He was quiet, reserved, and soft-spoken. I turned to Bob and said,

---

[11] Story by Shri Anandi Ma

"Jenny has accused you of not loving her and avoiding her day and night. Can you tell me your experience of this relationship?"

"I'm guilty of doing a lot of the things she says, but I do love her. Even though I love her, things between us are pretty bad. I stay away as much as I can, and try not to talk to her at home very much. As soon as I come in the door, Jenny starts screaming at me. She accuses me of not loving her, of being a bad husband, and all sorts of stuff."

I said, "What is it that you do that aggravates her so much?"

"For years I tried to talk to her, but she just attacked every statement I made, and she was so quick and aggressive, I'd get overwhelmed and just quit trying to answer her barrage of questions."

Bob and Jenny had a complimentary type of relationship. Each had strengths the other lacked. Bob needed help expressing himself. He was not as assertive, and he kept all his feelings to himself. Jenny was very expressive and wore her feelings on her sleeve. Bob obviously needed more of the expressiveness that came natural to Jenny. She could have benefited from Bob's ability to work internally with his feelings and stop blurting out every minor irritation. Each of them had weaknesses their partner held as strengths. Their relationship was a mirror for them to reclaim the very attributes they didn't like about themselves. Life was pushing them forward to either a point of self-awareness or further dissociation with their fingers pointing at one another

As we started couple's counseling, it was difficult for Bob and Jenny to stop blaming each other. Years of anger and resentment made it difficult for them to step back and observe their own personality shortcomings. One of the hardest things in a couple's life isn't that their partners are different from them; *it's that they don't accept their differences or see how they're meant to integrate their own lack of such qualities in many cases*, a concept that most find bewildering at first.

Once Jenny and Bob realized they couldn't change their partners by nagging and withdrawing, they were ready to listen to some new ideas. Each of them was willing to admit that they might benefit by absorbing the attributes their partners possessed that caused them so much aggravation. Implementing this concept was difficult because working with each other's attributes triggered their emotional issues. They struggled between believing they were mirroring each other, and angrily reacting or withdrawing when either of them expressed attributes that the other needed to internalize.

Bob would say to me, "Don, I know that I need to express myself better, but I can't stand up against that bag of wind over there."

My reply was, "You're doing a good job. Speaking out and defending yourself is foreign to you, but it beats running silent and infuriating Jenny. Just keep the name-calling out of it. Besides, you know that this quality was one of the things that attracted you to her, and you can't keep living like a mole digging a hole when things get tough. You probably met plenty of women like yourself, but we're attracted to our opposites so that we can face our weaknesses and incorporate what's missing. It's one of the basic rules of relationships. But they also cover up our greatest fears, so confronting them in others makes us angry and furious at times."

This stopped both of them as they thought through this concept. Jenny was the first to speak up. "Wow. I can see that. So, it's not others so much, as it's each of us dealing with our own shit." Bob laughed, wishing he could have expressed it as well. They were both beginning to understand Yogananda's teaching:

"Whenever you see wrong in others, and are distressed by it, remember it's the wrong within you. When you are right inwardly, all things are right, for you see everything as part of God. You then accept all things as they are, without judgment, and look with kindness and sympathy on everyone, no matter how foolish."[12]

Sometimes people ask me how long they have to work on themselves to achieve a higher state of consciousness. I tell them it is entirely up to them. Each opening leads to a greater submergence into the Godhead. It is limitless. It is infinite. The reward is now and later.

"What is found now is found then. If you find nothing now, you will simply end up with an apartment in the City of Death.

"If you make love with the divine now, in the next life you will have the face of satisfied desire."[13]

A Woodcutter Goes Forward

Once upon a time, a holy man met a simple woodcutter who was very devoted to God. The holy man said to him, "Go forward." On returning home, the woodcutter asked himself, "Why did the holy man tell me to go forward?" The next day he followed the advice and went deeper into the

---

[12] Kriyanda. *The Essence of Self Realization.* Kriyanda.p.184   Crystal Clarity Pub. Nevada City, CA 1990

[13] Bly, Robert *The Kabir Book #19.* A Seventies Press Book. Beacon Press. Boston 1977

forest. This time he discovered some valuable sandalwood trees. He was very happy and returned with cartloads of sandalwood, which he sold and became rich. He saw the holy man again and was told to go forward. He went deeper into the woods than before and discovered a silver mine near a river. This was even beyond his dreams. He dug out the silver and sold it at the market. He got so much money that he didn't even know how much he had accumulated.

A few days passed and he internalized what the holy man said, "Go forward." This time he went to the other side of the river and found a gold mine. Then he exclaimed, "Ah, this is what the saint wanted me to find." On returning home he realized that he was to go forward again, the message was now truly inside him. A few days later he went very deep into the forest and found heaps of precious gems. He took these gems home and became as rich as Kubera, the God of Wealth himself.

Whatever you may do, you will find better and better riches inside yourself if only you go forward in your practice. You may find a little peace if you meditate. Don't conclude, however, that you need not go any further than daily meditation. Go forward and reap the fullness of the boundless fruits awaiting you as you open to the kingdom of God within.[14]

In the next chapter, we will discuss how to raise consciousness by means of various spiritual practices. Understanding how our mind works accelerates the process. The reverse is particularly true: as we raise our spiritual

---

[14] *The Sayings of Sri Ramakrishna.* 1104 Sri Ramakrishna Math, Chennai 2003

consciousness, it helps us to know ourselves and to transmute the energy of the ego into spiritual attunement with the divine.

You Are Not a Single You

When you fall asleep, you go from the presence of yourself
into your own true presence.
You hear something
And surmise that someone else in your dream
has secretly informed you.
You are not a single "you."
No, you are the sky and the deep sea.
Your mighty "Thou," which is nine hundredfold,
Is in the ocean, the drowning place
Of a hundred "thous" within you.[15]

---

[15] Helminaki, Kabir. *The Rumi Collection*. Shambala Library, Boston. 2005

Chapter Eight
The Road to Ultimate Good

"If they say to you,
'Where did you come from?'
Say to them, 'We came from the light,
The place where light came into being of its own accord,
And established itself and became manifested through
    their image.'
If they say to you,
'Is it you?'"
Say, 'We are its children.'
If they ask you, 'What is the sign of your Father in you?'
Say to them, 'It is movement and repose.'"[1]

God is immanent in creation as energy and consciousness.
He is the energy manifested in all organic and inorganic
matter, which is also held in the consciousness of God. When

---

[1] *The Gospel According To Thomas*

I realize that this world and all the people and everything in it are suffused with God, I can choose to pray to the God in heaven, seek the God within myself, or experience God manifested in everything on planet earth.

People tell a beautiful story of Lord Krishna and Radha, who was the closest of all his followers because of her love and devotion to Him.

It once transpired that Krishna observed Radha sleeping. From each and every pore of her body, there reverberated the divine name "Krishna, Krishna, Krishna." Seeing her absolute devotion, Krishna was affected so intensely that he fainted. When Radha woke up, she saw Lord Krishna lying near her. From his whole being, there radiated her name: "Radha, Radha." She too then fainted in intense ecstasy. When the Lord woke up, he again observed the divine name pouring out of her body and the cycle continued.[2]

The message in Radha's story is that when we take a step toward God, He takes a step toward us. The first move is solely up to us. Once taken, the divine movement begins and lasts for eternity, or until our final absorption back into the Godhead. Spirit is the closest thing to us; it is actually the essence of our being, but can appear furthest away if we do not seek or acknowledge it. Spiritual values help show us the way out of world-bound absorption, when we pay attention to its callings. We will chase after material satisfaction, until our rational mind comes forward and asks,

"Is this all there is?"

"Is this all I want to settle for?"

The concept of God varies greatly depending on our

---

[2] June 07 Article *Exotic India*. Nitin Kumar

cultural and spiritual education. When asked, most people will tell you they have a soul, although their understanding of the word may vary greatly. Irrespective of whether the spiritual seeker is from the East or the West, the language of spiritual truth is the same.

"The kingdom is inside of you and it is outside of you. When you come to know yourselves then you will become known, and you will realize that it is you who are the living sons of the father."[3]

"I pray . . . That they all may be one; as thou, Father, art in me, and I in thee, that they may also be one in us: that the world may believe thou hast sent me."[4]

One of the oldest recorded stories of man's inquiry into the nature of God takes place between a twelve-year-old boy and death. This teaching has not changed through the ages and is found in the Katha Upanishad.

Nachiketas Holds Death Hostage

A twelve-year-old boy, whose father had given away all his belongings, asked his father if he had given him away yet.

"Father, have you given me to somebody?" After thinking a while, his father answered him. "I give you to Death."

The young boy named Nachiketas thought, 'Whether I die now or later matters little; but what I would like to know is what happens if Death gets me now.' Nachiketas went into the forest and sat in meditation within the house of Death.

Death said to Nachiketas, "A guest should be respected; you have lived three days in my house without eating and

---

[3] *The Gospel According to Thomas.* Ibid.

[4] *The Holy Bible.* John

drinking. I bow to you, take from me three gifts, and I will be the better for it."

Nachiketas said, "I will take as my first gift, that I may be reconciled with my father, that he will make me welcome."

Death said, "I shall so arrange things, that when your father gets you back, he shall sleep well at night."

Nachiketas next said, "Death, you know what fire leads to heaven, show it to me, I am full of faith. I ask that fire be my second gift."

"The fire that leads to heaven is your second gift," Death replied. "Now choose again the third gift."

Nachiketas said, "Some say that when man dies he continues to exist, others that he does not. Explain that and this will be my third gift."

Death said, "This question has been discussed by the gods, it is deep and difficult. Choose another gift, Nachiketas! Do not be hard. Do not compel me to explain."

Nachiketas insisted, "Death you say that the gods have discussed it, that it is difficult; what explanation can be as good as yours? What gift compares to that?"

Death said, "Take sons and grandsons, all long-lived, cattle and horses, elephants and gold, take a great kingdom. Take anything but this; take wealth, long life, Nachiketas. Take an empire, anything whatever; satisfy the heart's desire. Pleasure beyond human reach, fine women with carriages. But do not ask what lies beyond death."

"Destroyer of man! These things pass," Nachiketas said. "Joy ends, the longest life is short. Keep your horses, keep singing and dancing, keep it all to yourself. Wealth cannot satisfy a man. If he but pleases you, Master of All, he can live as long as he likes, get all he likes, but I will not change my gift. What man subject to death and decay, getting the chance of an un-decaying life, would still enjoy mere long life, thinking of copulation and beauty? Say where man goes after death: end all that discussion. This, which you have made so mysterious, is the only gift I will take."

Death finally said, "I will teach you then. The good are one, the pleasant another: both command the soul. Who follows the good, attains sanctity; who follows the pleasant, drops out of the race. The mind of the wise man draws him to the good; the flesh of the fool drives him to the pleasant . . . they are diverging roads: one is called ignorance, the other wisdom. Nachiketas, you turn toward wisdom. The fulfillment of all desire, the conquest of the world, freedom from fear, unlimited pleasure, magical power, all were yours, but you renounced them all, brave and wise man.

"The wise, meditating on God, concentrating their thought on him, entering the mouth of the cavern, discovering deeper in the cavern, that Self, that ancient Self, difficult to imagine, more difficult to understand, that passes beyond joy and sorrow. The man that, hearing from the Teacher and comprehending, distinguishes nature from the Self, goes to the source; that man lives forever, attains joy; in that joy, Nachiketas your gates of joy stand open.

"The Self knows all, is not born, does not die, is not the effect of any cause, and is eternal, self-existent, imperishable, ancient. The individual Self and the universal Self, living in the heart, like shade and light, and though beyond enjoyment, enjoy the result of this action. God does not proclaim Himself; He is everybody's secret, but the intellect of the sage has found Him. God, the inmost Self, no bigger than a thumb, lives in the heart."

Then Nachiketas, having learnt from Death this knowledge, rose above desire and death, found God. He who acts like Nachiketas finds Him.[5]

Nachiketas reasoned with Death and forced him to tell the truth. We have said many times that reason and spirituality are never in conflict, but they may appear to be at odds at lower levels of awareness. From prehistoric times, Eastern thought has taught that God is immanent in nature yet transcends creation.

The indigenous people of the Americas held the same idea of God as their brothers in the East. The American Indian embarked on vision quests to contact the Great Spirit. During his quest, he would quiet his ego through fasting, vigil, and sacred ceremonies to commune with God. He also considered the earth and all its creatures sacred. He understood God to be present in nature and also to be outside nature. The highest teachings of Vedanta and the unschooled learning of the American Indian are the same. We are the Microcosm of the Macrocosm. This belief of an immanent God has been experienced time and again by holy men and women in deep communion with God.

A Dominican monk by the name of Meister Eckhart was condemned to death by the papacy for his heretical beliefs. He experienced God in mystical union and wrote of his experiences. The Church Fathers of the time failed to comprehend Christ as alive, as passionately living and loving Himself through men and women. They believed that Jesus was outside the human realm, literally at the right hand of God, to be prayed to in heaven. Although Meister Eckhart died before his sentence could be carried out, he chose to live

---

[5] Yeats. *The Ten Principle Upanishads*. Katha Upanishad. Faber & Faber 1985 London

his truth at a cost of his own life as Jesus and Socrates had before him. His writings survive to this day.

Eckhart said, "God gives birth to the Son as you, as me, as each one of us. As many beings—as many gods in God. In my soul, God not only gives birth to me as His son, He gives birth to me as Himself, and Himself as me.

"I find in this divine birth that God and I are the same; for in this birth, I have become the motionless cause of all that moves. I have won back what has always been mine. Here, in my own soul, the greatest of all miracles has taken place— God has returned to God!"[6]

The message of Nachiketas, from about the fifth century B.C., and the experiences of Master Eckhart in the thirteenth century are much the same. They both found God deep within the recesses of their own being.

Yoga, Path to the Divine

The word yoga translates into "union." Yoga practice is the means by which we unite with God. There are different yoga disciplines to suit different individuals. Hatha yoga, widely practiced in the United States, is preparatory yoga. It strengthens the body so that one can remain healthy and vigorous in order to sit in meditation but is not a yoga discipline of union. The main systems of yoga are Bhakti Yoga, Dhyana Yoga, Karma Yoga, and Jhnana Yoga. (As I elucidate these Eastern Yoga systems, know that each form of devotion or selfless service has its equivalent in Judaism, Islam, and Christianity. Since my study for the last fifteen

---

[6] Harvey. *Teachings of the Christian Mystics.* P.92 Shambala. Boston 1998

years as been mainly Eastern, this is a natural reference point for me.)

Bhakti Yoga

Bhakti Yoga is yoga of love. It is a real, genuine search after the Lord, a search beginning, continuing, and ending in love. The person connects with the love of God by loving God either as God manifested in man or in one of his incarnations like Jesus, Krishna, Ram, or the specific form of his belief.

Kabir, author of most of the poems in this book, was a Bhakti yogi. His poems are suffused with the love of God. St. Theresa of Lisieux, known as the Little Flower in Catholicism, practiced a form of devotion similar to a Bhakti Yogin. As she helped the aged, infirm, and sometimes irritable sisters of her order, she saw herself helping God.

One doesn't have to be a saint or ascetic to follow Bhakti Yoga or any of the yoga systems, or their Western equivalent. This path of devotion and service is followed widely in both the East and the West. It is the yoga of selfless love. Angelina Jolie has given millions of dollars to disenfranchised refugees and brought their cause to the international public's attention by adopting several children from such camps and speaking out on their behalf. She practices her own form of Bhakti Yoga.

There are different forms of bhakti worship; however, one point remains the same. *The love of God must be pure and not for earthly benefit.* Sometimes those who love in this manner receive positive recognition and are honored by our society. They need to be mindful not to let their ego claim the good work they have accomplished. Love given in this manner begets love from the divine. It is love for love's sake with no attachments. Attachment debases it and puts a ceiling on the experience of the pure love of God.

Krishna said, "He sees himself in the heart of all beings and he sees all beings in his heart. This is the vision of the yogi . . . And when he sees me in all and he sees all in me, then I never leave him and he never leaves me."[7]

Most adults do not experience a personal love for God. As with any experience we need to cultivate bhakti through spiritual practices. In India, devotees of Gopal, the infant Krishna, talk to the child and bathe and dress the infant statues. In their temples the infant is given food, flowers, and fresh clothes daily. We don't do this in America, but it is a devotional practice one can do with the infant Jesus or the deity of choice. If you care to place a candle before the image, give it fresh flowers, and talk to it, before long you will experience a presence emanating from the image. It will come alive for you in your home and in your heart. Your bhakti will be returned in ways you cannot imagine.

Another practice that develops love for God is to sit in front of a picture or statue of Jesus or any religious picture or image and say the following:

Dear Jesus, I respect you,
I allow you to respect me,
I honor you,
I allow you to honor me,
I accept you,
I allow you to accept me,

---

[7]   Mascaro.*The Bhagavad Gita.* 6. 29-30 Penguin Clasics. 1980. N.Y.

I love you,
I allow you to love me,
I am one with you,
You are one with me.

This is a powerful practice. As with all daily meditation, practice yields the greatest benefit. I suggest you do this twice daily for ten minutes.

Ramakrishna, a great Hindu saint of the 19th century, was assigned as a novice monk to take care of the altar at Dakshineswar in Calcutta. Part of his job was to place fresh flowers and fruit at the feet of the Holy Mother. His duties also included performing intricate ceremonies that had been part of the Hindu religion for centuries. Because of the intensity of his devotion, he fell into trances at times and failed to always complete his duties. The following account tells of the deep ecstasy he experienced as a Bhakti Yogi.

Ramakrishna described his first vision of the Mother: "I felt as if my heart were being squeezed like a wet towel . . . Suddenly my glance fell on the sword that was kept in the Mother's temple. I jumped up like a madman and seized it, suddenly the blessed Mother revealed herself. The buildings with their different parts, the temple, and everything vanished from my sight, and in their stead I saw a limitless, infinite effulgent Ocean of Consciousness. As far as the eye could see, the shining billows were madly rushing at me from all sides with a terrific noise, to swallow me up . . . within me was a steady flow of undiluted bliss, altogether new, and I felt the presence of the Divine Mother."[8]

---

[8] Nikhilananda *The Gospel of Ramakrishna.* p.14

Many saints, East and West, have described similar experiences. In the fourteenth century, a young girl named Catherine of Sienna tried to imitate the Fathers of the Desert and would withdraw into solitude to the dismay of her parents. If anything grieved her, it was the loss of her solitude. In her eighteenth year, she became a nun in the order of the Dominicans. For three years it is said that she never spoke to anyone but God. She gave her heart completely to God and experienced Him in her soul.

She wrote, "O abyss! O eternal Godhead! O deep sea! What more could you have given me than the gift of your very self? You are a fire always burning but never consuming; you are a fire consuming in your heat all the soul's selfish love; you are a fire lifting all chill and giving light. In your light you have made me know the truth: You are that light beyond all light who gives the mind's eye supernatural light in such fullness and perfection that you bring clarity to the light of faith."[9]

Catherine, like Ramakrishna, loved God with all her heart. Their experiences of ecstasy, although phrased in the language and culture of their time, were almost identical. The love expressed in the brief vignette of Radha and Krishna was for both of them a personal experience.

The stories of saints seem extraordinary, somewhat removed from our daily life in the West, and one can have difficulty identifying with them. More than one person has said to me, "I'm not Mother Theresa; I couldn't think of doing what she did." I tell them she is a model of devotion for us to emulate in our own way while living a secular life in

---

[9] *Teachings of the Christian Mystics.* Ibid. P. 121

the West.

Bhakti is a very simple universal path of devotion. In words reminiscent of Kabir, George Herbert wrote,

"Teach me, my God and King,
In all things thee to see,

And what I do in anything
To do it as for thee.

All may of thee partake
Nothing can be so mean

Which with his tincture, 'For Thy sake,'
Will not grow bright and clean."[10]

The treasure is everywhere. God resides in everyone and everything. If you do not see it, offer everything you do with love to God and you will experience His love in return as St. Francis of Assisi did.

The daily repetition of the prayer of St. Francis is a practice that will increase your love of the divine. I suggest reciting his prayer four times a day: morning, noon, evening and bedtime.

Lord, make me an instrument of your peace.
Where there is hatred, let me sow love;
where there is injury, pardon;
where there is doubt, faith;

---

[10] Ibid. 133

where there is despair, hope;
where there is darkness, light;
and where there is sadness, joy.

O Divine Master, grant that I may not so much seek
to be consoled as to console;
to be understood as to understand;
to be loved as to love.
For it is in giving that we receive;
it is in pardoning that we are pardoned;
and it is in dying that we are born to eternal life.

Teilhard de Chardin wrote, "Some day after we have mastered the winds, the waves, the tides, and gravity . . . we shall harness the energies of love. Then, for the second time in the history of the world, man will have discovered fire."[11]

Dhyana Yoga

Dhyana Yoga is the yoga of meditation. The Buddha wrote the *Satipatthana Sutra*, which is a discourse on concentration and mindfulness. He says that the mind is not easily controllable because it wanders "hither and thither." He recommends focusing the mind to gain one-pointedness because it is "a mental state common to all."[12] Typical points of focus are at the tip of the nose, the forehead between the eyes, and on the heart.

---

[11] Teilhard de Chardin. *The Phenomenon of Man.* Harper Colophon Books 1965

[12] Narada. *The Buddha and His Teachings.* Satipatthana Sutras. Buddhist Pub. Society, Kandy 1980

Maharishi Patanjali, considered the father of yoga, gave detailed instruction in the *Yoga Sutras* on meditation:

Yoga pose is a steady and comfortable position.
Yoga pose is mastered by relaxation of effort
Lessening the tendency for restless breathing,
And promoting an identification of oneself
As living within the infinite breath of life.
Contemplation is the confining of thought to one point.
Meditation depends upon the foundation of directing thought
Into a constant flow of awareness. [13]

The sage Patanjali deals with one of the problems a beginning meditator experiences. When a beginner sits to meditate, his mind typically experiences a flood of thoughts.

Both the Buddha and Patanjali recommend focusing attention on one point of the body. The most frequent points of focus are the third-eye center above the eyebrows, the tip of the nose, and the heart. This provides a focal point for the active mind to return to between thoughts. The mediatator gazes on the focal point, loses it as a thought comes, and then refocuses. Another aide in quieting the mind is to repeat a sound quietly in one's mind such as "Om," which emits a quieting vibration. Slow relaxed breathing quiets the mind.

Many people start to meditate and give up because their mind is flooded with thoughts. They also may not continue because they force themselves to meditate too long, get

---

[13] *Yoga Sutras of Patanjali*. 11. Stiles. Weiser Books, Canada 2002

bored, or don't experience anything from their meditation.

Many beginners expect immediate spiritual results after meditating a short time. This is contrary to the manner in which we learn. Whether learning a trade or studying for a profession, we spend long years and countless hours gaining experience. Meditation is not an exception to that rule. However, most of us do experience subtle results such as peace, less stress, a sense of well being and so forth. False expectation can deter anyone from learning anything. Meditation is no exception.

Patanjali makes four points to help the beginner: a) sit comfortably, b) breathe in a relaxed manner, c) focus on a point to steady the mind, and d) remember that you are identifying with the infinite breath of life.

I would add to that list, don't be in a hurry for spiritual experiences. My recommendation is that beginners start with five or ten minutes a day. I suggest they concentrate on relaxing deeply by sitting comfortably and letting the breath do its work quieting the mind. Whether the mind is busy or not is unimportant. They should sit only as long as they feel relaxed and then get up feeling refreshed. As they continue this practice, they can sit for longer periods of time if they follow the basic principles of meditation.

When the mind is quiet, the ego is put on hold. You are what's left—the you that existed before this birth, and the you that will continue when the body ceases to exist. When you experience quietude, you have touched the surface of beingness. As you continue with meditation, you move deeper and deeper into Self. This movement is deliberate and slow for most of us. Meditation practices position you to experience the infinite depth and infinite potentiality within yourself, which ultimately leads to profound experiences with the Self. The experiences of meditation at this level urge you forward so that you can't wait to start your next practice.

Another way to meditate is to silently repeat a mantra such as Om Nama Shivaya when you are sitting in a relaxed manner, breathing comfortably, and focusing your attention. It translates, "I am one with you Lord God." The mantra contains sounds that are healing and quieting to the mind.

Om Nama Shivaya tapes are offered through the Internet. This mantra is relaxing to listen to when you are not meditating and the vibrations work at subtle levels of consciousness as well.

Meditation is not solely confined to the East. There is a very old Christian meditation known as the Jesus Prayer. The individual closes his eyes and centers his focus on his heart and silently repeats, *"Jesus, Son of God, have mercy on me"* or *"Jesus, Son of God, love me."* One can add the second phrase as the heart stirs you. This prayer will open the heart to the love of God. The following is a brief primer on the Jesus Prayer by Nicephorus, Patriarch of Constantinople, written in the eighth century.

"You know that our breathing is the inhaling and exhaling of air. The organ that serves for this is the lungs that surround the heart. Thus breathing is a natural way to the heart. And so, having collected your mind within you, lead it into the channel of breathing which air reaches your heart and let your mind descend to the heart and remain there. When you thus enter the place of the heart, as I have shown you, give thanks to God and, praising his mercy, keep to this doing, and it will teach you things that in no way will you ever learn. Moreover you should know that when your mind becomes firmly established in the heart, it must not remain there silent and idle, but it should constantly repeat the Jesus prayer, "'Lord Jesus, Son of God, have mercy on me.'"[14]

In the East, people who meditate repeat the Jesus prayer like a mantra. Monks of the Eastern Church repeat it silently throughout the day. I suggest trying to say this mantra throughout the day for just one day. You will notice a change.

The experiences of meditation are widely varied. Each of us is unique and will not have identical experiences. God is infinite; therefore, mediatators will experience difference aspects of the Godhead with no two ever having identical experiences. Even when they follow certain traditional patterns, each individual will express those experiences in a unique manner.

Vivekananda writes, "When man reaches this state beyond ordinary human knowledge through prodigious effort, if it is not part of his belief system then, in one country it will be seen as coming through an angel, in another through a deva, and in a third through God. What does it mean? It means that the mind brought out the knowledge from within itself and that the manner of finding it was interpreted according to the beliefs and education of the person through which it came. The real fact is that these men came upon, as it were, upon this super-conscious state."[15]

When one thinks of spiritual practices, mediation comes to mind. It is not the only path to experience our inner divinity. Each of us is unique and therefore the method that suits one of us does not suit all of us. Other paths will take you to the Self as well.

---

[14] *The Sayings Of The Desert Fathers*. Cistern Pub. Kalamazoo Michigan. 1984

[15] *The Gospel of Ramakrishna*. Ibid. P.14

Karma Yoga

Karma Yoga is the yoga of selfless action. The Karma Yogi offers all his actions to God. The following vignette underscores the importance of this yoga.

A young brother asked one of the elders, "There are two brothers, of whom one remains praying in his cell, fasting six days at a time and doing great penance. The other one takes care of the sick. Which one's work is more pleasing to God?"

The elder replied: "If that brother who fasts six days at a time hanged himself by the nose, he could not match one who takes care of the sick."[16]

Mother Theresa was a Karma Yogin. She taught her novitiates to set their ego aside so the grace of God could work through them. She followed in the footsteps of Karma Yogins before her. In the sixteenth century, a young girl by the name of Theresa of Avila wrote,

"Christ has no body like yours,
No hands like yours, no feet but yours,

Yours are the eyes through which is to look out
Christ's compassion to the world;

Yours are the feet with which he is to go about doing
    good;
Yours are the hands with which he is to bless men now."[17]

---

[16] *The Sayngs of the Desert Fathers*. P. 42. Cistercian Pub. Kalamazoo, Michigan. 1984

[17] *Teachings of the Christian Mystics*. Ibid. P.183

Mother Theresa was Christ in action. Her words were virtually identical with the name of the saint she took when she received her vows. She was His feet, hands, eyes, and heart. Many asked how the sisters could perform such work under dark depressing conditions. When I was at her nunnery in Calcutta, I saw a sign on the wall that gave the answer. "Make yourself small so He May become large." She was Christ serving the Father by working with the poor and dying in the slums of Calcutta. She fed and bathed them and made them comfortable in her home. When they died in her hands, they took her love with them on their journey. She lived the sage's teaching.

"All actions take place in time by the interweaving of the forces of Nature; but the man who doesn't understand thinks he himself is the actor."[18]

"No work stains a man who is pure, who is in harmony . . . 'I am not doing any work,' thinks the man in harmony who sees the truth; he remembers 'It is the servants of my soul that are working.'[19]

"Whatever you do, or eat, or give, or offer in adoration, let it be an offering to me ...and with thy soul one in renunciation thou shalt be free and come to me."[20]

St. Paul spoke to the Corinthians: "Whether therefore ye eat or drink, or whatever ye do, do all in the glory of God."[21]

Vivekananda practiced the various yoga paths and had this

---

[18] *The Bhagavad Gita*. Ibid. 3-27
[19] Ibid. 5-8
[20] Ibid. 9-27
[21] *Holy Bible*. St.Paul Corinthians

to say about Karma Yoga:

"It is a difficult thing in this world to work and not care for the result, to help a man and never think that he ought to be grateful, to do good work and at the same time never to look back to see whether it brings you fame or nothing at all. Even the most arrant coward becomes brave when the world praises him. A fool can do heroic deeds when he receives the approbation of society; but to constantly do good without caring for the approbation of his fellow man is indeed the highest sacrifice he can perform."[22]

I've found in my experiences that the ego clings to praise. The gains achieved by an individual in psychotherapy are truly gains wrought through effort. I am pleased when someone makes progress, but am also able to accept lack of progress with greater equanimity than earlier. My ego still likes to claim the successes but I find it easier to acknowledge the Wisdom that did the work. A greater challenge for me is when people graciously thank me. Although I remind myself that the good they received is from the divine within, my ego still likes to gloat on praise. To deal with this challenge, I have taken Krishna's words to heart, offering the results of my work to God. Through my experience I believe this is the easiest way to practice karma yoga.

Krishna told Arjuna in *The Bhagavad Gita* that he was not the doer. He didn't have to worry about winning or losing. His karma was to follow. Krishna told him that if he couldn't dis-identify from doer-ship, then to do his best and make his work an offering to God. "Set thy heart upon thy work, but

---

[22] Vivekananda *The Yoga & Other Works*. P. 45 Ramakrishna/Vivekananda Center 1984 N.Y.

never on its reward . . . be free from selfish desires, be not moved in success or failure"[23]

I like mantras or phrases that help us to remain centered. When we repeat them often enough, they become a part of our thinking. The following is easy to learn. "It is the divine in me that helped you, not the me you see." Repeat this silently; otherwise you flaunt your spirituality before others. If you work at this, you will sooner or later get a glimpse that the Christ in you is working through you.

Every spiritual teacher I have studied tells us that God accomplishes His work through us. I found it interesting that more than a century ago, Ramakrishna, a great saint of that era who had little formal education, had this to say about the ego well before the founding of psychology. I have never heard the term "ripe" or "unripe ego" before reading the following:

"Those who seek name and fame are under the delusion. They forget that everything is ordained by the Great Dispenser of all things and all is due the lord and the lord alone. The wise man says, 'It is Thou, O lord, It is thou;' but the ignorant and the deluded say, 'It is I; It is I.'

"Nothing is mine, whatever I see or feel, or hear nay, even this body itself, is not mine: I am always eternal, free and all knowing—*such ideas arise from the ripe ego.* This is my house, this is my child, this is my wife, this is my body,"—thoughts of this kind are the manifestations of the unripe ego . . . *the Universal soul and the Universal Being are separated because of this unripe ego.*

"If you find that you cannot drive off this feeling of 'I'

---

[23] *The Bhagavad Gita.* Ibid. 2:47

then let it remain the servant, 'I.' There is not much to fear from the ego which is centered in the thought, 'I am the servant of God'[24]

St. Theresa's words can help remind us to be a Karma Yogi:

"Christ has no body like yours,
No hands like yours, no feet but yours,
Yours are the feet with which he is to go about doing good;
Yours are the hands with which he is to bless men now."

I think the most practical way to be a karma yogi is to follow the ideas set forth by the saints in this section by offering the selfless work you do for others as an offering to God.

Jhana Yoga

Jhana Yoga is the yoga of the discriminating mind, called the Yoga of Knowledge. The path of knowledge is a path to God.

The Buddha was a Jhana Yogi. In his discourse on the four noble truths, he taught an intellectual path to truth. As with all great teachers, he experienced a merging of the different paths and encouraged practicing each of them. Upon his awakening he taught the following truths:

Truth one, all beings suffer.

---

[24] *Sayings of Ramakrishna.* P.48 Ramakrishna Math. Chennal. 2003

Truth two, the cause of suffering is desire.

Truth three, there is an end to suffering called Nirvana.

Truth four, the Noble Eightfold Path leads to Nirvana.

The key element of the Noble Eightfold Path was "right understanding." Clear vision or right understanding leads to clear thinking. He taught that through knowledge and awareness one ascends the spiritual ladder. [25]

In the last chapter, we discussed Jhana Yoga. We learned that there are different levels of perception. When we step back from our stream of thoughts and emotions, we enter the witness state of consciousness. We let thoughts pass as if we are watching them on a screen.

A further step builds on the witness state of consciousness. If we reflect how our mind works, we realize that each thought we think, from the first thought we have as infants to the current thought we are experiencing now, has given us a sense of identity. Each emotion we experience from infancy to the present time and each interpretation of our behavior we made consciously or unconsciously formed a concept of who we are. Our sense of self is a contiguous association of thoughts, emotions, and interpretations. Who I am is more than the work I do. It is more than the relationships I engage in. It is more than any role I play or hat I wear. However, this complete panorama of memories and reflections defines our selves in our current existence at an ego level of awareness.

The eternal Self is the backdrop of awareness on which these impressions can be viewed. The Self is real. Jhana Yoga

---

[25] The Buddha and His Teachings. Ibid P.67

is learning to understand that the constructs of our world are mental phenomena and that only the Self is eternal. This is what the Buddha spoke of when he said right understanding leads us from suffering to Nirvana. The Jhana Yogi knows this and lives this understanding. He uses his ego to navigate the vicissitudes of planet earth, but is always aware of his eternal nature, his divinity.

At dawn, May 4, 1908, a young man by the name of Sri Aurobindo was confronted by the British police, guns in hand, to arrest him for attempting to kill the British Magistrate of Calcutta. The young man was thirty-six years old at the time. The police had confused him with his brother, Barin, who was a militant fighting British rule. Barin had actually made a bomb to detonate in the minister's palace. Sri Aurobindo was a very spiritual man and was somewhat confused as he waited in the Lal Bazar police station. Finally his court date appeared and he went before the magistrate. All stood at attention as the judge passed sentence. He was sentenced to one year in prison for the attempt on the minister's life. Sri Aurobindo hung his head as the judge read the sentence. He reflected how several months earlier he had the strongest intuition to spend some time in silent retreat. He followed his inner prompting and went into spiritual solitude. He wondered if his recent spiritual practices might have prepared him for more than a jail sentence.

As he reflected on this thought, he looked up and gazed first at the judge. In place of the judge, he saw a resplendent divine being. He next glanced at the clerk, and saw a divine being emanating from the clerk. As he glanced around the room, he saw God everywhere. Vasudeva, his personal God, had taken the form of police, attorneys, and everyone in the courtroom. Everywhere he looked, he saw God! Sri

Aurobindo was absolutely startled. As he entered his jail cell, with all sense of duality now having been swept away, he began working on a plan to reach others and instill in them this Truth.

Years later he built an ashram in Pondicherry where he developed a large disciple following and brought students close to God.[26]

Vivekananda made the following statement: "The world which you have conjectured was based upon a very partial experience, upon very poor reasoning, and upon your own weaknesses. Give it up. The world we have been thinking of so long, the world we have been clinging to so long, is a false world of our own creation. Give that up. What existed was the Lord Himself and Him in you."

"Please give up this dualistic vision of nature, the concept of friends and enemies. See everyone equally. *Our great and only enemy is our uncontrolled mind. Besides this enemy, there are no other enemies* . . . Seeing enemies and believing nature is dualistic is only due to ignorance." [27]

Jesus said, "When you do this to the least of my brethren, you do this to Me."

Jesus advises us how to live as a Jhana Yogi. See everyone as the Lord, treat everyone as you would treat the Lord, and love them as you do the Lord. Look for their essence, ignore the behaviors of their ego mind, for that is not who they are.

In the section on Karma Yoga, we said that the karma yogi

---

[26] Satprem. Sri Aurobindo, *The Adventure of Consciousness*. The Institute for Evolutionary Research. N.Y. 1984

[27] *The Yoga & Other Works*. Ibid. P.614

offers all his work to God until he reaches a stage where he is beyond ego. The Jhana Yogi sees everyone as God. He sees the play of the ego but perceives the Self in each individual. Therefore, the practice of Jhana Yoga is to offer everything you do, speak, or think to that person as God. A phrase like, "I offer this gift, help, aid, etc. from the God in me to the God in you" is a practical way to practice this yoga.

The teaching is the same, East or West. Jhana Yoga, as do similar Christian and Sufi practices, bring love and peace, and ultimately lead to a merger with the divine.

Four Paths or One?

It should be apparent that the Jhana Yogi who sees his brother as divine also loves Him, or that the Karma Yogin has bhakti for the people she helps. The paths interweave. Depending upon our disposition, one path may be easier to embark on than another, but sooner or later we find them merging. As one becomes more spiritual, no matter what the path, one expresses more of the soul, which is the Godhead of love, compassion, light, wisdom, and service to others. It is the fount of a pure potentiality because it is infinite. You can share in that infinity because your Self is infinite. You create your total reality; your mind is clay in the hands of the self. Set your ego aside and allow the creator within to create your reality.

A great King by the name of Vipaschit was about to leave his body and enter the heavenly realms. The angels and devas were very excited because he had been a very wise king, and they wanted to invite him to be their teacher. In the meantime the king passed through various ethereal realms and settled into his new spiritual abode. He was greeted with smiles and embraces and tears of gratitude. There he found joy and love many times greater than his earthly experience. One day he mentioned to a friend, "Heaven is wonderful; I never imagined so much love and joy." His friend said to him, "O great king, what do you mean, this is not heaven, it is hell. The people here were miserable before your arrival, but now they are filled with love and joy." Just then a retinue of celestial angels arrived apologizing profusely for having mistakenly placed him here, and they told the king to come with them. Vipaschit looked around and said, "I have found heaven; I am happy here and I plan to stay."[28]

Vipaschit, as ruler of a great kingdom, had practiced the various yoga paths and created a reality for himself that was so powerful it transformed the hell around him. Your creation is still unfolding. You know the tendencies of the ego and the potential of inner wisdom. You can choose a path that suits you and experience the infinite love, wisdom, and power within you.

The four paths to God are time-tested ways to experience the Divine in this life. They can be practiced by adherents of all religions because they are nondenominational. They transcend creeds and sects. They are simply spiritual practices, which saints of all faiths and religions have found beneficial in their search for the divine. No energy is ever wasted in this pursuit because the effort exerted in finding God is returned tenfold.

"Don't go outside your house to see flowers.
Inside your body there are flowers.

---

[28] Easwaran, Ekanath. *The Dammapada*. P.216 Nilgiri Press. Canada 2007

One flower has a thousand petals.
That will do for a place to sit.
Sitting there you will have a glimpse of beauty
Inside the body and out of it,

Before gardens and after gardens."[29]

As you walk your path, the divine presence inside of you knows everything and will direct you appropriately. Along the way you will meet *elephantine beliefs* that blind you to what is truly happening. If life doesn't dish up what you expect, reevaluate your approach and change. Don't ignore common sense. Remember there should be no conflict between spiritual aims and life's practical necessities. On the other hand, don't confuse realities.

You will find that the *King Chandrasena inside you loses faith* and gets angry at life. Discouragement will set in at times when everything doesn't run smoothly. Allow yourself to experience the vicissitudes of life. The lows can be just as beneficial as the highs. Trust that all your experiences have a meaning for you.

When you are most vulnerable, *the Asuras will try to convince you that Indra is wrong*, that the body is the self. They will tell you to pleasure yourself or wait another day to become more conscious. Like Indra, know that the Self is the imperishable within you, that which sees the reflection in the water, not the reflection itself.

Sticky Hair will demand that you be flexible and find

---

[29] *The Kabir Book*. Ibid. P.36

wisdom within yourself, and *not rely on outmoded means from the past to deal with current challenges* and *sticky* situations. *Prince Five-Weapons* hopes you will learn from his mistakes and *not rely on your ego to solve problems* but call upon the *resources of your higher self.*

If you listen carefully, you will find *that Jesus, Buddha,* Mohammed, *or Lord Krishna is your guide.* You can hear their message clearly when you are *quiet and turn everything over or offer your work to* God.

Self Depreciation and *Self Conceit* are *very much as dangerous as Sticky Hair.* They fly under your radar much of the time. So you need to ask yourself, "How do I feel about this action?"

The Ghost of Greed will try to lure you. It will tell you life is hard, and that you must take what you can. It's every man for himself. It doesn't share and it doesn't care. Scarcity is its motto. Sadly, it doesn't know that *everything comes from the ever-expanding cornucopia of the Infinite.*

Life will be your mirror and help you to know yourself. When you blame or find fault in others, Brother Pior will tell you that you are merely *mirroring* a part of yourself. Learn to read its reflection. Don't let shame or fear stop you. We are all human and fallible. Part of the process is making slip-ups, learning from them, and trying again. We make a lot of mistakes; *we are not the mistake.* Don't let feelings of inadequacy or negative self-judgments stop you from knowing your highest Self.

A twelve-year-old boy named Nachiketas had the same wisdom as the twelve-year-old messiah from Nazareth. Pay attention to them. Be like the woodcutter who went deeper and deeper into the woods and himself, and found diamonds while listening to their message.

It's a rare privilege to be a human being. Each day is a

precious gem. Consider yourself a guest on this planet and always treat others like your personal guests. The way will come to you because you are the way.

Chapter Nine
The Reality of Balancing Ego and God

In every age and on every continent God has spoken to us. Those that were spiritually adept knew how to listen. Sacred teachings that were ancient before man placed them on parchment bore the same message reiterated today:

Consciously or not, ignorant or not, we create renewal and change for the good of all of us – or – its opposite – annihilation. Mahatma Ghandi told us, "You must be the change you wish to see." His desire to change freed the Indian Empire from British rule. His thoughts and actions liberated a nation through peaceful means.

On an opposite continent across the Pacific Ocean, when the Mahatma was empowering his movement, another Indian, a Pueblo Chief by the name of Ochwiay Biano, told Carl Jung we needed to respect the deepest wisdom within us:

"We are people who live on the roof of the world,
We are sons of the sun, who is our father.

We help him daily rise and cross over the sky.
We do this not only for ourselves,
But for the Americans also.
Therefore they should not interfere
With our beliefs.
But if they do so and hinder us,
Then they will see in ten years
That the sun will rise no more."

Ochwiay Biano was steeped in ancient wisdom. His appreciation for the sacredness of the creation had been imprinted in his DNA for tens of thousands of years. His cathedral was the open sky. His grandfathers spoke to him through cloud formations whose language he understood before man had developed the written word. Sacred ceremonies, never revealed to the white man, took place in the Kiev as elders contacted their gods. Transcendental wisdom through vision quests gave them knowledge of what was to come as well as how to guide their lives. Their knowledge of the interwoven fabric of all that exists was a truth that had been handed down for millennia. Their dance was God's and God's dance was their dance and dancer and dance were one.

They lived this truth until we broke our treaties and lied to them. We converted the American Indian into a cerebral religion that held no heart for them. In place of the sun, earth, and sky we gave them a barren reservation. We changed sacred earth into real estate earth and hung a price on it. Through our spiritual ignorance and intellectual arrogance we extinguished the light that had been undimmed for eons. The wisdom that lasted from the dawn of time until a short while ago darkened. New gods replaced the old.

Casinos and the greenback replaced their sacred vision as we dimmed the light of their consciousness.

No doubt we had split the atom and were sending rockets to the moon. Yet in our ego indulgence we were spiritual primitives. Native Americans held the light. Our graven images were money and possessions. *They taught us that man cannot be torn apart from his soul. They knew that outer man and spiritual man must dance together to survive.* Our head was full of ideas, our hearts closed—we couldn't understand their language because they knew how to listen to the Voice in the heart.

We didn't know that they danced for us as well. We didn't understand that life was a sacred weaving and that an action here had a consequence there. The light of consciousness that dwelt in the heart was replaced by ideas. The complex interweaving of man and God as dance and dancer co-creating reality was replaced by the greed and ignorance of indulgent egoism.

They knew that the heart which moves in love, acceptance, compassion, understanding, sensitivity, and generosity is the seat of God.

When Ochwiay Biano was asked about the difference between the white man and Indian, he replied, "The white man thinks with this" —pointing to his head, "we think with this" —pointing to his heart."

Fifty years later I found myself looking at the pueblo dwellings carved from ochre colored earth. They were arranged along rows from the bottom of the cliff to the top. It was still possible to climb the cliff and enter their dwellings. My friend Doug and I did just that. I entered row after row of dwellings, stopped briefly to bask in the sun and then climbed more. Finally I reached the upper most dwellings, and after visiting them, climbed to the top.

Not far from where I stood was a huge circular opening in the ground. To my astonishment I had come across a Kiev, their sacred ceremonial enclave. I called to Doug and we climbed into the Kiev. It was carved out of the sandstone in perfect circular fashion. A few pieces of burnt wood lay where some traveler probably spent a cold night keeping warm. Otherwise the Kiev was empty.

Doug and I performed a brief ceremony and then closed our eyes. As we paid our respect to those that came before us we climbed down the cliff. Half way down I decided to rest once more on the sandstone shelf in front of a dwelling.

With my eyes once again closed a voice said to me, "It is good to rest and nurture your self." I replied, "You weren't in the Kiev, it was cold and empty, I couldn't feel your Presence." The voice said, "You can only rest here, you can't go into the past, the past is over. My fire is now in your heart, it is time that you teach what you know."

Ochwiay would not have been surprised with the events that followed his prophecy.

He didn't live to see that our Asian policy of containment took us into Vietnam in the 1950's and ultimately cost three to four million Vietnamese and American lives.

He didn't live to see that the scourge of drugs that followed our soldiers home from Vietnam mentally crippled millions of young Americans and is a battle we continue to lose.

He didn't live to see that our obsession for oil caused us to invade Iraq under false pretenses and start a war that alienated the Muslim Nations.

He didn't live to see that we had the audacity to dismiss Islam, as we did his religion, as inferior, and attempt to convert these peoples to a rigid judgmental distortion of the teachings of the Christ.

Ochwiay didn't live to see that our bankers and leaders with whom we trusted with fiduciary responsibility succumb to greed and avarice on a scale so huge that it took the United States and the world economies to the brink of depression with unimaginable suffering for millions.

As with all spiritual teachers he would have reiterated that we have a choice. The Voice will always direct us when we develop ears to listen. We can learn to listen to our hearts and touch the sacred within as we honor the sacred in others. We can learn from *Princes and Ogres* and other such teaching books. We can use our intelligence with genuine humbleness and gentleness to seek the greater good for all. We can choose to touch the fount of universal wisdom and love layered beneath our consciousness or we can continue to behave as we have in the past.

When we arrogantly dismiss the spirit within and seek to assuage the ego with greed and inhumanity towards our neighbors, we play with forces that we do not fully understand. The American Indian understood that life is a sacred weaving that must be approached with the greatest humbleness and respect. A movement here causes a movement there. Our thoughts and actions create vibrations that reverberate around the planet.

Ochwiay was an ordinary Plains Indian, but the Voice within roared through him as it did every spiritual and consciousness teacher throughout mankind's history.

His people were not dreamers. They were practical dwellers of the Midwest. They planted crops, dug irrigation, harvested, built homes, and educated their children to survive on the vast plains they called home. They made weapons, fashioned cooking instruments, and spent their lives involved in mundane everyday tasks.

They were in touch with the sacred within themselves and without. Nevertheless they integrated daily life and its humdrum tasks with a respect for the sacredness of the creation. They integrated God and ego. They knew what each called for and respected their complete humanness and godliness. Although they never heard of Jesus, they lived his teaching. "Give unto God that which is God's, and to Caesar that which is Caesar's."

They had much to teach us. Now more than ever we must question the needs of the ego and balance our legitimate needs with deep wisdom so we bring healing and peace to ourselves and our planet.

Princes and Ogres has taught that our egos may swell to immense dimensions as depicted by Sticky Hair—full of arrogance, cruelty, and inhumanness or just as readily shrink to smallness, fear, and insecurity. Whether our unchecked ego inflates or deflates itself, it always projects our inner thoughts on to the world and creates divisiveness and worse.

All of us must take on the ogre within and deal with its wily nature. As Indra taught us, the ego is not the Self yet it has legitimate needs that require attention. We need appropriate shelter, food on the table, a circle of family or friends that support us, personal relationships that are mutually fulfilling, and other such needs. These desires are healthy and important to each one of us.

We are reaching a point where each misstep and each miscalculation can have catastrophic consequences for all of us. Global warming and nuclear proliferation are just a few of the issues that imperil our planet.

Ochwiay Biano invites us to dance on the top of the world

by weaving nature, ego, and transcendental wisdom into a fabric of beauty, love, and respect for the sacredness that lies deep within all of us. *Princes and Ogres* has shown the practicality of the perennial spiritual wisdom that has been handed down from millennia.

My professional life has been dedicated to helping others heed the needs of the ego and answer the spirit within. We must attend to both. Just as we cannot disregard the message of Ochwiay, Ghandi, and legions of sages from every culture and every land we cannot disregard the human tasks we face in a post technology, post computer, post internet, and post virtual world in which we live. This is our reality and we cannot escape from it into pseudo mysticism or get caught in spiritual bypassing, ignoring our realities and the stresses that bear upon us.

I believe that our world is changing faster than our ability to adapt to it without undue stress. Our nervous system changes slowly. We must live in a world that calls upon us to deal with stresses that would have been unimaginable before the industrial revolution, yet our brain has not changed much since we tilled the fertile Nile Valley in the Neolithic Age.

We have much wisdom to guide us. The messages from our teachers bear the imprint of perennial truth, but I believe we need to know how to apply these truths in a meaningful way to our lives. The science of psychology can help us to nurture and strengthen our emotional and mental selves. We need to integrate psyche and spirit so we can once again ride the sun across the sky as we Twitter and text one another.

We create renewal and change each and every day of our lives. We cannot escape the fact that our choices and decisions deeply affect each other and planet earth as well. We have the ability to consciously create a harmonious, loving world while manifesting our humanness and spirituality. Over and over again we learn that outer man cannot be ripped apart from his sacred consciousness without crushing ourselves and our loved ones and desecrating our planet.

Will you take the challenge and help the Sun cross the sky?
You are the sun.
Will you help yourself?

Index

C

D

E

H

heaven, **99**, **210**
hell, **126**, **135**, **210**
   personal, **62**, **132**
Herbert, George, **193**
Hildegard of Bingen, **77**
Hindu, **4**, **191**
Hinduism, **114**
holy war, **5**
Homo sapiens, **60**
human, **10**, **12**, **25**
   behavior, **4**
   beingness, **3**
   condition, **12**, **31**
   experience, **46**
   humanness, **10**
   nature, **25**

I

India, **8**, **10**, **15**, **30**, **50**, **119**, **162**, **183**
Indian Land Reform Movement, **31**
Indra, **50–52**, **59**, **211**
I-ness, **55**, **80**, *also,* Self
Iraq, **218**
Iron John, **4**
Islam, **189**, **218**
Islamic, **4**
issues
   universal, **5**

J

James, William, **119**

K

L

M

---

meditation, **47**, **48**, A

B

D

H

heaven, **99**, **210**
hell, **126**, **135**, **210**
    personal, **62**, **132**
Herbert, George, **193**
Hildegard of Bingen, **77**
Hindu, **4**, **191**
Hinduism, **114**
holy war, **5**
Homo sapiens, **60**
human, **10**, **12**, **25**
    behavior, **4**
    beingness, **3**
    condition, **12**, **31**
    experience, **46**
    humanness, **10**
    nature, **25**

I

India, **8**, **10**, **15**, **30**, **50**, **119**, **162**, **183**
Indian Land Reform Movement, **31**
Indra, **50–52**, **59**, **211**
I-ness, **55**, **80**, *also*, Self
Iraq, **218**
Iron John, **4**
Islam, **189**, **218**
Islamic, **4**
issues
    universal, **5**

J

James, William, **119**

K

L

M

N

O

P

T

Acknowledgements

Roughly five years ago, my Vedic Astrologer, Pravinji, suggested I write a second book. I always paid attention to messages that came through dreams, synchronicities, and unexpected other mediums. The language of the unconscious is never explicit and leaves room for interpretation. This time my intuition confirmed the message, and I knew exactly what to write. I wanted to teach in the ways used before the printing press was discovered. The method of imparting lessons with stories to anchor important life themes dated back to prehistoric times.

It wasn't long before I started writing that I needed some professional guidance. A writer-friend introduced me to John Nelson, who was familiar with the ideas I wanted to express. John was particularly helpful in encouraging me to express my ideas without reservation, which I did, without whitewashing the concepts.

John also introduced me to Devra Jacobs, a book agent who read the manuscript with a keen eye and suggested some important changes. Devra helped me reduce the psychological jargon and use more teaching stories to keep the book readable and interesting.

As an unknown writer, I needed to find a publisher. American Book Publishers liked the manuscript and took a chance. Andrew Frame, my copy editor, suggested changes to the chapter titles to create greater appeal. I found working with Andrew very helpful and am appreciative of him and American Book Publishers for bringing Princes and Ogres to fruition.

Katy Day has been a friend for many years. Katy is the type of person who will tackle any task and is unafraid to learn about it while trying. I decided to see how good she really was and asked her to develop an index for me. Katy persisted and presented me with a very professional index.

I have learned a great deal from my psychotherapy clients over the last fifteen years. Their stories are in here, as teaching lessons, to demonstrate that anyone has the power to change their lives. The line between teacher and student gets blurred much of the time, and I am indebted to everyone who crossed the portals to my therapy office.

My family has been very supportive. I am blessed with the finest daughters that have walked the face of the earth. Their love, a ray of divine love, has fostered my personal growth as much as anything I can think of. My grandchildren, in their innocence and beauty, reflect how we all are beneath our shields of protection. They inspire me to write about your pristine beauty beneath the layers that separate us from your authenticity.

Women in my life have been most influential. My mother comes to mind first. She loved me and stood by me when most mothers would have killed me as a kid. She imparted to me a sound sense of morality and told me God was watching. Little did I know that God was inside me, taking note of every breath I took and secretly stewarding my life.

Carol, my wife of ten years, has provided me with opportunity to know myself in a way no one else could. She holds a mirror up to my nonsense and I have learned more about myself in these years than I did in the previous sixty. We are connected in soul. I cannot share how I come by this knowledge, but it is so. We are united, one spirit, at the highest level of our conscious existence. At the level of our daily awareness, we get to enjoy the privilege of being together to enjoy and respect one another as only can be done in physical reality.

Shri Ananda Ma is my spiritual teacher. I had been meditating for many years before I meet Ma, but through her teachings and personal help she has ripped open doors to the sacred within me that lifetimes of spiritual practice could never have done. I have come to understand natural law, which is spiritual law, and how to break free from the chains that keep us from experiencing beauty, love and joy.

To my teacher, Shri Ananda Ma, I owe her infinite lifetimes of service to God and man.

About the Author

Don Mordasini is a graduate of the University of California, Berkeley. He enrolled in Graduate School at the Institute for Integral Psychology in San Francisco seeking to expand his knowledge of psychology with the idea of integrating it with Eastern Wisdom.

He practiced Theravada Buddhism with a renowned teacher and studied western psychology. As he started practicing psychotherapy he met his guru, Shri Anandi Ma. He remains her student to this day, visiting India annually to be with her in meditative retreats deepening his experience of the sacred.

He has been co-owner of Los Gatos Therapy Center the

last fifteen years. He works with individuals, teaching them to weave the sacred into their daily lives as they grapple with life's daily challenges.